All my best,

[signature]

Capital Attraction

Capital Attraction

[The Small Balance Real Estate
Entrepreneur's Essential Guide
to Raising Capital]

Matthew Burk

Advantage®

Published by Advantage, Charleston, South Carolina.
Member of Advantage Media Group.

ADVANTAGE is a registered trademark and the Advantage colophon is a trademark of Advantage Media Group, Inc.

Printed in the United States of America.

ISBN: 978-1-59932-592-7
LCCN: 2016934565

Book design by Matthew Morse.

This publication is designed to provide accurate and authoritative information in regard to the subject matter covered. It is sold with the understanding that the publisher is not engaged in rendering legal, accounting, or other professional services. If legal advice or other expert assistance is required, the services of a competent professional person should be sought.

Advantage Media Group is proud to be a part of the Tree Neutral® program. Tree Neutral offsets the number of trees consumed in the production and printing of this book by taking proactive steps such as planting trees in direct proportion to the number of trees used to print books. To learn more about Tree Neutral, please visit **www.treeneutral.com.** To learn more about Advantage's commitment to being a responsible steward of the environment, please visit **www.advantagefamily.com/green**

Advantage Media Group is a publisher of business, self-improvement, and professional development books and online learning. We help entrepreneurs, business leaders, and professionals share their Stories, Passion, and Knowledge to help others Learn & Grow. Do you have a manuscript or book idea that you would like us to consider for publishing? Please visit **advantagefamily.com** or call **1.866.775.1696.**

Acknowledgments

The acknowledgment segment is the one section of most books I read that I consistently tend to skip. Now that I have written a book of my own, I realize that, ironically, it is the section likely to be the most personal to the author. I have long said that I would write a book someday, but "someday" always seemed to really mean some day other than today. Given all of the other things going on in my life, it has been very easy to find many perfectly good reasons not to do it, as I'm sure is true for most authors. To finally do it has only come about with the encouragement, help, and support of many people who deserve mention. I believe all of these people know that I feel more strongly about them than the limited number of words I am using here can convey. I will, however, make the effort anyway, knowing it will not be fully adequate to express my feelings.

In no particular order, I am very grateful to the following individuals and companies:

- Lance Pederson, for his unique and intellectually stimulating business mind and acumen
- Darris Cassidy, for his drive, ambition, and likability
- Jay Zollinger, for his level-headed, wise, and practical counsel and dry sense of humor
- Angie Henderson, for being my right-hand deal person for twenty years and counting

- Kellen Stevens, for leaving to find out that coming back was right for both of us
- Wally Glausi, for his advice and guidance and for helping, in many ways, to make me the fund manager I am today
- Earl Nightingale, whose sage observations delivered in his baritone voice changed the course of my life
- Stephen Covey, whose ideas resonate deeply with me and permeate my beliefs and actions
- Ron Huntington, for his coaching, encouragement, and business wisdom
- Robert MacLellan, for his creativity and ideas, his timely mediation, and his entrepreneurial zeal
- Entrepreneurs' Organization, for being the single most influential organization I have ever encountered and exposing me to most of the ideas, people, and experiences that have contributed to my development as a businessperson
- All of my EO Altius Forum mates, past and present, for your ideas, your passion, your friendship, and your unconditional and nonjudgmental support through some very trying times
- John Brooke, may you rest in peace, for some of the most powerful and intense experiences and lessons I ever had
- Frank Landini, may you rest in peace, for teaching me how to be a real estate lender
- All of my investors, past and present, for entrusting me with your hard-earned money and—especially those in Funds IV and V—for your patience, support, and calm during a storm
- Pat Terrell, for helping me make Fund VII a reality
- MC Rydzewski, for pushing me to get this work completed and helping to get it to the finish line

- All of my fund-advisory clients, for helping me to learn everything that follows even more deeply by allowing me to teach these concepts to you
- My parents, for believing in and supporting me long enough to get me on the right track and for putting up with me when I'm sure I was pretty hard to put up with
- My grandfather, Ben A. Burk, for being pretty much exactly what a grandfather should be
- Other people, in no particular order, for supporting me and Fairway over the years and/or otherwise motivating me in one way or another and thus contributing to my ability to create this work: KC Reinhart, Mike McNaughton, Barry Johnson, David Ambrose, Jeff Spiegel, Adria Wright, Erica England, Victor Paru, Advantage Media Group, Verne Harnish, Craig Russillo, Chet Holmes, Jim Rohn, Fred Baldwin, Craig Bressman, Dodd Clasen, and many others who, if not named here, still have my appreciation for whatever lessons and experiences they brought to me

Finally, I could not have devoted the many hours of effort and work it took to write this book without the support of my family, particularly my wife, LaRae, who is everything I could ever ask for in a partner in life, and my sons, Ben and Brody, who I hope will someday be inspired to write a book on something that is equally as personal and important to them that can in turn inspire and assist others.

Contents

Introduction

Raising money from other people to fund your real estate deal is hard. Raising money continuously from other people to regularly and repeatedly fund multiple real estate deals inside a pooled fund over which you have full autonomy and your investors have none is even harder. Anyone who has ever done any sort of real estate deal using other people's money knows this to be true. Those who have made a *business* out of doing real estate deals using other people's money and who must raise capital every day know it even more deeply. And every one of them has considered to one degree or another how to do it better, more efficiently, and more effectively. It is for these people, those I call small balance real estate (SBRE) entrepreneurs, that this book has been written.

In 1992, only one year after leaving my native California, where I had lived my entire life, the company that had relocated me to Portland, Oregon, closed eighteen of their twenty-one offices, including the newly opened Portland branch they had sent me off to launch, and I was out of a job in a foreign place. So I did what any self-respecting wannabe entrepreneur does and started my own company. Since I had no money, literally, I borrowed $10,000 from American General Finance Company at a less-than-attractive interest rate of 21 percent and started a mortgage brokerage company. Since that time, I have originated both prime and subprime residential loans, funded them on warehouse lines and sold them on the secondary market, left that business to move entirely into private hard money lending, originated or acquired more than a thousand SBRE deals, serviced a portfolio of hundreds of private money loans, and launched and ran seven pooled investment funds. The great majority of these deals has been funded with capital we raised ourselves from private investors.

Among my many experiences in the twenty-three years running my own SBRE business, two of them stand out as being, by an order of magnitude, the most difficult and most impactful on the direction my business and life have taken. They were very much intertwined, and they both occurred during the period of time now known as the Great Recession. Many people in the real estate business have deeply painful stories of how that economic meltdown affected them, some of which involve the loss of their entire life's work and savings, so I do not pretend mine are any more brutal than some other people's. However, they impacted both my personal and business lives deeply and took me and my company, Fairway America, to the brink of financial distress. They required me to persevere through greater adversity than I had ever faced and to dig deeper into my own resourcefulness than I knew I could go. In the process, they allowed me to transform what I was doing professionally in a way that has given rise to Fairway's current business model, a model that greatly exceeds anything my prior model would ever have been able to achieve. As Einstein said, "Adversity introduces a man to himself."

The first experience was taking on a business partner in early 2008. By 2007, I had successfully funded many hundreds of hard money loans, operated three successful funds, and built up a loan-servicing portfolio north of $50 million. Raising capital to fund these loans was, however, still very challenging and time consuming, and I felt I had the ability to originate even more quality loans than I had the capital to fund. An acquaintance of mine, John, who had recently sold his company for an eight-figure number approached me about buying Fairway. I told him I didn't want to sell but was looking for some additional firepower in being able to raise capital more consistently and effectively. (Aren't all SBRE entrepreneurs? This is probably why you are reading this book!) Long story short, after several months of negotiation and due diligence, I sold John 50 percent of the company and we embarked upon what we expected to be a seven-year plan to build the company. He wrote me a sizeable check on January 1, 2008, and we were off and running.

On February 15, just forty-five days later, I got a call from John on my cell phone as I sat with a friend of mine having a glass of wine late on a Friday afternoon. I was leaving the next morning with my family for a vacation in Palm Desert, partly to get out of the damp darkness of a Portland winter and partly to celebrate having had a nice financial outcome as I embarked on the next phase of my business life. I will never forget that conversation as long as I live.

"You know that hernia?" John said to me. (He had been having some low-back pains and thought he had a hernia.)

"Yeah, what about it?" I said.

"Well, it isn't a hernia."

"What is it?" I asked.

"The Big C."

"Cancer?"

"Yes."

"How bad?"

"Stage 4," he said, as he started to cry on the phone. He was forty-one years old at that time.

That day began what was to be a grueling twenty-two-month ordeal that took his life on December 21, 2009.

The other experience was every bit as difficult and impactful to the company, though in a different way, as John's struggle with cancer, facing his own mortality, and ultimate passing. In September 2008 when he was battling cancer, John and I made the fateful decision to accept a large credit facility from Wells Fargo Capital Finance (WFCF) of $50 million. The line had a three-year maturity and was to come due in August 2011. From the very beginning, I was hyper-aware of the maturity date of that facility and the need to extend or replace it when it came due. As market conditions (along with my partner's) deteriorated, I communicated early and often with WFCF to make sure they were on board. "Of course we are" was the answer I always got, an answer so often given by bankers to entrepreneurs just prior to them actually not in fact being on board any longer. Despite the bank's reassurances up until the eleventh hour, there were ever-increasing signs that they were wavering. Their willingness to fund deals that met our underwriting criteria, deals which were much, much harder to come by as the market worsened, became increasingly unreliable. As we went to renew the line in the late spring of 2011, their tune really began to change, and to make a long and painful story short, they would not renew the line on terms that we could meet without blowing our loan covenants.

As any entrepreneur who is too heavily weighted in a single supplier, a single customer, or a single vendor understands, such a heavy reliance on that single outside source for a vital component of your business—material, sales, or, in my case, capital—can place the entire enterprise at risk. This was the risk that I knew we had run when we took on this credit facility in the first place, but I believed at that time that as long as our assets performed, which they largely did throughout the downturn, we would be able to extend or replace the line. Certainly by September 2008 when we signed the deal, I also sensed there was to be a significant downturn in real estate. But I felt having access to very inexpensive capital would provide us with a strategic advantage in the marketplace for hard money loans. Unfortunately, I did not anticipate the magnitude of the financial crisis and subsequent downturn—the Great Recession—and how completely it would transform the financial and real estate worlds. Ultimately, the bank's refusal to renew that line on similar terms to what they had originally provided and our inability to find a replacement, which quite simply did not exist in 2010 and 2011, precipitated the most difficult business decision of my life, the one to wind down our fund whose assets I had spent the last decade systematically building.

These were the darkest times of my life. Real estate values had dropped precipitously. Delinquencies were at record levels. Borrowers were routinely calling us asking for the "bailout package" (literally). The number of mortgage brokers in the marketplace, along with loan origination volume, was down more than 80 percent. I had no access to capital and no ability to generate income from new loan originations, which had been my livelihood for the past two decades. I had to terminate several longtime and valued employees in order to cut overhead. My business partner was dead from cancer at the age of forty-three. And now I had to go tell all my investors I had spent years developing and building trust with that they were not going to be getting any money anytime soon and that we were going to embark on a systematic wind down of the fund. What did that mean to them, not to mention to us? How would we pay them back? What could I say to them, and how could I continue to earn their trust? How would we originate any new loans? Even if we could, where would the capital to fund them come from? How could we actually make any money? How would the company survive? At the age of forty-seven and facing the potential failure of my business and the loss of all that I had worked so hard for the past almost twenty years, what would I do now? These were the thoughts going through my mind in the summer of 2011.

For many years before this, I had long held the belief that it is not what happens to a person that matters but rather how they respond to those circumstances that is important and that defines them. It is not when everything is going well and things are rosy that character is revealed, but rather it is when you are facing extreme circumstances and difficulties that you come face to face with what you are really made of. This is very easy to say and believe when things are good, as they had been for me for a long time. It is a much more difficult belief to hold when you are facing business failure, potential bankruptcy, and total loss of reputation. I was now at that point, and I knew that how I responded would be a testament to my character and resilience and would define me to my employees, my investors, and myself. It was from this position that I was to subsequently reinvent Fairway's business model and, in many ways, myself. To get great answers, one must ask great questions. To ask great questions, often one must have no other choice. Necessity is truly the mother of invention, and it allowed, even forced, me to pursue new directions that have resulted in a business that has completely transcended anything I'd ever done before. Where I was in 2011 isn't a place I ever want to be again, but if I hadn't been forced by a combination of circumstances and events, some within my control and some not, to go there, I would not be in the position I am today, and I would not be writing this book.

Over the past two decades and particularly in the past four years since we reinvented our business model, I have learned a tremendous amount about how to build a small balance real estate business, grow a company, and raise capital from high-net worth individuals in order to do real estate asset-based deals with a goal to build wealth for them as well as myself. All that I have learned is from being directly in the fray, doing some things right, making many mistakes, and always trying to do the right thing and to learn how to do things better. Along the way our business has grown and shrunk and morphed in ways I could never have predicted and has given me a deep understanding of the space we call "small balance real estate." From deal structures to underwriting to raising capital to accurate administration, there are several critical elements to nail when creating and running a high-quality SBRE business that is attractive to the right capital sources. I hope in the following pages to share some of this understanding with you to help make your journey easier.

A WORD OF CAUTION

Virtually every aspect of being an SBRE entrepreneur raises questions that have significant legal, accounting, and regulatory implications: Do I need a license to make a loan secured by this single family residence? Do I need to verify that this investor is accredited before I can accept an investment from her? How do I value the assets in my fund for purposes of determining how much I need to pay to redeem this investor? The answers to these kinds of questions can be very complicated and will likely be different for each SBRE entrepreneur, based on their specific asset model, investment structure, and location.

Although it would be impossible for this or any other book to answer all of the complex legal and other questions each SBRE entrepreneur needs to have in order to succeed, some of what I say in this book does touch on certain aspects of a few of those questions. My lawyers tell me that I need to make it clear from the outset that **I am not an attorney or a CPA, and I am not qualified to give any kind of legal, accounting, or other professional advice that requires a license.** Whenever I touch on legal or accounting issues, please understand that I am not offering any professional advice—I am merely sharing my understanding of certain issues from a business perspective.

Although my understanding of these issues has been informed by my conversations with my own advisors over the course of my career, **no one should rely on anything I say as legal, accounting, or regulatory advice.** Instead, if you want to raise any money from investors to help fund your real estate activities, you need to develop a strong relationship with a great attorney, CPA, and other advisors as needed. Although there is certainly a short-term cost to involving professional advisors in your business, obtaining good professional help is an absolute necessity to being successful in this space and, over the long run, the benefits of that advice will be invaluable to you.

Chapter 1

What Is an SBRE Entrepreneur?

Since it is for these people that this book has been written, I think a good place to start our discussion is to attempt to define exactly what I mean by a "small balance real estate entrepreneur." Stated simply, my definition of an SBRE entrepreneur is *anyone running a business whose basic function is to make and manage noninstitutional grade and sized investments in one or more real estate asset-based strategies requiring the operator to regularly and consistently raise capital in order to make those investments.* This definition eliminates a lot of "real estate" people from it by its nature, including real estate agents, homeowners, appraisers, property managers (who don't also raise capital and invest), and anyone I would categorize as "institutional," such as large hedge fund managers, REITs, pension funds, banks, and other market participants who play in the more institutional and less entrepreneurial space.

To further clarify, let's put some additional general parameters around "small balance real estate." Broadly speaking, I would consider SBRE to be anything where the average deal size is $5 million or less, and in the vast majority of cases $2 million or less. In fact, in a very large percentage of SBRE businesses, the average deal size is less than $1 million or even $250,000. I know many of what I would consider to be full-fledged SBRE entrepreneurs running SBRE businesses with average deal sizes below $100,000.

When it comes to a pooled investment fund, which is the capital structure I discuss in great deal in this book, I would loosely define an SBRE fund as one with total assets under management (AUM) below $500 million, more frequently below $200 million, and the vast majority of the time below $100 million. There are many perfectly good, well-run, and profitable (for both the investor and our SBRE entrepreneur) funds that have total AUM of $10 million or $20 million or $50 million. In fact, I know and work with many SBRE entrepreneurs transitioning from the syndication model of raising capital and starting SBRE funds literally from zero. In many ways, this is the person for whom this book will likely be most helpful.

The total volume of real estate transactions in the United States is very difficult to estimate, even when just limiting the criteria to actual sales of real property. The volume of real estate transactions when you include not only real property sales but also the financing and refinancing of such property, the sale and trading of real estate secured debt instruments (trust deeds, contracts, tax liens, and others), and other transactions that have real estate as the underlying asset is almost impossible to calculate. I believe it is safe to say that this figure is in the trillions of dollars.

If we remove all of the owner-occupied single family residential sales and refis from the total, and we remove all of the institutional sized deals, such as the sales and refis of Manhattan (or other major metropolitan area) office towers, regional shopping malls, large industrial complexes, and other properties that are outside the scope of my definition of SBRE, we start to narrow down our universe to the SBRE realm, and it is still a gigantic market by any measure. For example, Boxwood Means' monthly report, the Small Balance Advocate, estimates a total sales transaction volume in the United States of what they call "small cap commercial real estate" of more than $58 billion year to date through August 2015. This does not include *any* single-family residential investment property transactions, which, by most cursory research I have done, is another multibillion-dollar market. This also does not include *any* private or hard money lending volume on both residential investment and commercial income-producing property, another multibillion-dollar market. This also does not include *any* buying, selling, and trading of distressed or discounted real estate secured notes in the private markets, another multibillion-dollar market. And this does not include *any* other strategy involving real estate as the core collateral or asset of that strategy, of which I am personally familiar with many (since I speak with them every day of my business life and many are Fairway's clients).

SBRE	Institutional
Deal sizes < $2 million	Deal sizes > $25 million or more
Institutional capital unavailable	Fund sizes > $500 million
Highly fragmented	Small number of large players
Wide variety of strategies	Compressed yields
SBRE funds < $100 million	Tried and true strategies
High yields	Scalability required
Customized fund structures	Minimum investment allocations too large for SBRE entrepreneurs
Difficult to obtain market data	Economics/terms dictated to SBRE

While the small balance real estate industry is clearly a gargantuan market collectively, it is also highly fragmented and highly regionalized, even localized, making it difficult to characterize and less sexy to the media. The vast majority of the media attention in the real estate field is on the institutional players, focused on Blackstone, Zell, Colony, Goldman Sachs, CalPERS, Wells Fargo, and similar multibillion-dollar companies, institutions, and funds. Yet most of these institutions want little to nothing to do with small balance real estate unless they can deploy a minimum of $50 million or $100 million at a time, and that usually is just a starting point. There are many reasons for this, but the net effect is that the SBRE industry functions much like a parallel universe to the institutional real estate world. Things that work well in one world, especially as it pertains to the way in which capital is accessed, often do not work at all in the other. This is an important dynamic to accept, as it has big implications to SBRE entrepreneurs.

The distinguishing factor to me about an "SBRE entrepreneur" versus other people who make their living in the real estate field is not the particular strategy you are pursuing but rather whether or not your business requires you to raise capital from others on an ongoing basis in order to execute that business strategy. If it does, then you are an SBRE entrepreneur. If you run a business operation of which some portion must be dedicated to systematically raising capital to support the development and growth of that enterprise, you are an SBRE entrepreneur. The significance and importance of developing systems, processes, and expertise in this capital-raising component of an SBRE entrepreneur's business is, unfortunately, very often underestimated and/or overlooked by most of them, and thus the ability to execute in this area is generally far less developed than the "deal" side of the enterprise. This becomes a fundamentally limiting factor in your growth and development unless and until you effectively deal with it, and many never do. Understanding and methodically improving this capacity is the focus of this book.

Having had to raise capital for Fairway's deals and pooled investment funds for close to twenty years, I have learned the hard way what works and what does not. I have also had the opportunity in the last three years to work as an advisor, mentor, and coach to more than a hundred SBRE entrepreneurs on this topic. At the same time, Fairway is actively using the ideas, strategies, tools, and tactics you will learn about in this book to raise money for our current proprietary funds. Throughout the remainder of this book, I share with you what I believe are the most important elements in building an SBRE business that can systematically attract the capital you need to build and grow that business.

TYPES OF SMALL BALANCE REAL ESTATE ENTREPRENEURS

One of the things that always fascinates me about the SBRE industry is the sheer variety of ways there are to make money in it. There are literally tens of thousands of SBRE entrepreneurs executing dozens of strategies on all types of real estate all over the United States, ranging in size from a handful of deals per year to many hundreds. Let's spend a few minutes discussing the primary and some secondary profiles of SBRE entrepreneurial business models.

Private Lenders

One of the most common SBRE entrepreneurial endeavors is being a private, non-bank lender, also known as "hard money" lending. Hard money or private money lenders originate loan opportunities from people seeking to borrow money to acquire (or refinance) property for a variety of reasons and who cannot qualify for or don't want to deal with obtaining financing from a bank. There are multiple variations of private, hard money lenders, including construction, development, commercial, and bridge lending (not all mutually exclusive). The private lender locates, underwrites, and arranges the closing of the deal and often then collects the payments and manages the loan through any default and/or foreclosure on behalf of the investor. Doing any significant volume of these types of deals requires substantial amounts of capital from investors on an ongoing basis. How this capital is raised may differ from one lender or broker to another—ranging from one-deal-one-investor-at-a-time to fractionalizing (multiple investors in one deal at a time) to a pooled investment fund (many investors investing in an entity that originates many deals, with both investors and deals coming and going at various points)—and is a focus of this book.

Private lending is actually a very large industry unto itself. I myself have been a private lender for many years, and this is where I cut my teeth in the real estate asset-based business. There is much to like about this business and much to dislike, but it is a classic example of an SBRE entrepreneurial enterprise. Raising capital is a critical component to success, and yet many if not most are regularly frustrated with that aspect of their business, as it is not what they enjoy doing. The best private lender entrepreneurs, however, make the commitment to get as good at this aspect as they are at the "deal" side of the business, for which they are almost always more naturally suited and inclined. I use this industry and business model for many of my examples throughout this book.

Fix-n-Flippers and Buy-n-Holders (Single Family Residential)

Many people enter the real estate investment business by purchasing a house in disrepair with the intent to fix it up and either sell it for a profit or rent it out for a return on their investment while they allow it to appreciate. This is probably the simplest, most common, and widespread model of real estate investing in the United States. There are a huge number of people who become involved in real estate in this manner, the vast majority of whom will do one or a few houses here and there on the side while working some other full-time occupation. Then there are those who turn this into a full-fledged business and do this on a much larger scale, actually making a living out of it. Some of these will do a handful of houses per year, and some will do dozens or more per year or even per month, turning this activity into a true enterprise. This requires a significant amount of capital on a regular, ongoing basis and meets my definition of a SBRE entrepreneur.

This business has always been around and has flourished over the past six or seven years. Many large institutional players have become involved in this business and many more SBRE entrepreneurs have as well. They will often borrow from private lenders for a portion of their capital but still need the equity component in addition to the debt. The interplay between this category and private lending is tightly knit, but these are two distinctly different SBRE entrepreneurs, each of whom has a more or less endless appetite for capital if their deal volume is strong. Fairway has literally dozens of clients involved in this space who are at various stages along their journey, ranging from doing a few deals to doing hundreds and even thousands of homes per year. How they capitalize their enterprise is central to their growth pace, their size, and their operations. I talk a lot about this group as well.

Value Add and Opportunistic Real Estate (Multifamily and Commercial)

Another common SBRE entrepreneurial investment strategy I see frequently is what I will refer to simply as "value add." This is basically the same model as the fix-n-flip/buy-n-hold outlined above but applied to commercial and multifamily real estate. The strategy is to locate poorly managed, neglected, and/or underperforming real estate—usually due more to the ineptitude of the owner/manager than to inherent shortcomings of the property, although these can sometimes be confused—and to provide the attention, capital, and expertise necessary to improve the condition, operations, and cash flow in a way that exceeds the investment necessary to achieve that end and thus realize additional value for the SBRE entrepreneur (often called a "sponsor" in this model) as well as the investor(s). Sponsors in this category will often focus on a particular real estate asset class and get particularly adept at locating, negotiating, and perpetuating off-market, distressed situations that meet their under-writing criteria. Some of the more common asset classes upon which sponsors will focus are multifamily residential (the most common), retail, office, self-storage, light industrial/warehouse/flex, hospitality, and other, more specialized asset types.

This can be a lucrative strategy if executed and applied well, and there are a lot of serious, talented, and experienced SBRE entrepreneurs in this category. These people have the same fundamental challenges as SBRE entrepreneurs in other categories in that they require significant amounts of capital on an ongoing basis in order to execute this business model. The manner in which they obtain this capital, the structure of that capital, and the skills and abilities they possess to do so effectively vary tremendously and play a very large role in the ultimate size, scale, and scope of their enterprise.

Distressed/Discounted Note Acquisition

Another entire field or industry of SBRE entrepreneurs focuses not on the direct acquisition of real estate, nor on the origination of new financing for people who cannot or do not want to deal with banks or other traditional lending institutions but rather on the acquisition and trade of existing loans and liens secured by real property. This would include performing loans, subperforming loans, and nonperforming loans, as well as other liens on real property (judgments, tax liens, etc.), in both senior and junior positions. The price paid for the assets will vary widely depending on a variety of factors, including the amount of the lien relative to the perceived property value, the payment history on the loan, the seasoning of that payment history, the position of the lien in the capital stack of the property, the face rate of interest, the maturity date, the amount of senior or, to a lesser degree, junior encumbrances, the location and demand for the real estate, the loan and the property's cash flow, the perceived compliance or lack thereof of the borrower, and many more. Often the strategy is to acquire the note securing the property and to ultimately foreclose or otherwise obtain title to the property and then apply the value-add strategy to it.

This can be a complicated, specialized, and often very lucrative business but also a potentially dangerous one for the less experienced. In this business, as in the fix-n-flip business, many people new to real estate will start by trying to buy a note at a discount and use their own capital to do it. A much smaller number of people actually make a true business out of it by doing it regularly, repeatedly, and extensively. This requires them to raise capital on an ongoing basis in order to execute the business model and therefore makes these people SBRE entrepreneurs.

Others

While the previous categories, of which there are multiple variations of each, are the most common, there are any number of other real estate asset-based strategies that require capital on a recurring basis whose operators may also be considered SBRE entrepreneurs. A few examples that I have seen and worked with include:

- **Tax lien certificates**—the acquisition, management, and disposition of tax lien certificates, including foreclosure and REO disposition as needed
- **Lease to own**—the acquisition of SFRs with the intent to lease to a long-term tenant and provide them an option to buy the property at a specified price in the future
- **Fractional interests**—the purchasing of fractional interests in property, similar to time share or vacation rentals
- **SFR acquisition via other methods**—including bankruptcy trustee, foreclosure auction, HOA liens, etc. with intent to rehab, rent, resell, etc.
- **Build to suit**—construction of commercial real estate that is preleased to a particular tenant
- **And more...**

At the end of the day, if you are running an enterprise whose basic strategy for making money is derived from an involvement in real estate that requires you to raise capital systematically in order to execute that strategy, you are probably an SBRE entrepreneur.

UNIQUE FACTORS TO SBRE ENTREPRENEURS

There is another unique component to an SBRE entrepreneur's enterprise that does not exist for entrepreneurs in most other industries, such as retail, services, technology, marketing, and many others, that makes superior performance over time difficult. Investing in real property, or loans or liens secured by property, carries performance risk that changes over time as market conditions cycle (see chapter 5). The value of the assets being originated or acquired by the SBRE entrepreneur on behalf of his investors can and will fluctuate over time, and therefore their long-term performance is only known after significant time periods have elapsed. Often there can be inherent problems (or opportunities) embedded in the assets owned at any given moment that are not readily apparent to the investors from whom the SBRE entrepreneur is seeking capital—and even to the entrepreneur himself.

"If you are running an enterprise whose basic strategy for making money is derived from an involvement in real estate that requires you to raise capital systematically in order to execute that strategy, you are probably an SBRE entrepreneur."

In addition, depending on the capital structure of the SBRE entrepreneur's enterprise, about which we talk a great deal more in chapter 4, there are quite often inherent conflicts of interest between our entrepreneur and his investors. This is largely due to the fees he will earn by simply doing more deals, regardless of market conditions. Frequently the fees, or at least some portion of them, are being paid at the time the deal is being done, *independent* of the long-term performance of the asset(s) being acquired. Therefore the incentive, economically at least, for the SBRE entrepreneur may be to do deals whether they perform or not. Of course, smart, honest, and disciplined operators will do all they can to ensure strong long-term performance for their investors because obtaining capital from these investors is necessary to their business model, as my definition of SBRE entrepreneur explicitly requires, and strong performance is usually a prerequisite to be able to continue raising capital. Market conditions can often exert their own will on that performance, however, despite the best intentions and efforts of the SBRE entrepreneur. How that entrepreneur responds to such developments also goes a long way toward long-term success or failure in raising capital.

All of this contributes to the complexity of running a truly successful SBRE enterprise over the long term. Managing these dynamics effectively, and many others I discuss in this book, is the challenge that all SBRE entrepreneurs face, and, as in many professions, only a few can master all of them. Raising capital is at the heart of what connects these otherwise disparate groups and becomes in many ways the constraining force of their business. And this gives rise to the Small Balance Real Estate Dilemma.

Chapter 2

The Small Balance Real Estate Dilemma

Running your own blind pool fund is a vision, a dream, and an aspiration of many SBRE entrepreneurs. The idea inspires. "I'm going to run my own fund someday." I have heard it many, many times from friends, clients, and others I know in the industry. As sexy as it may seem, a pooled investment fund capital structure is an order of magnitude more complex on multiple levels and in ways that cannot fully be known until you are managing such a vehicle. I like to use the analogy that launching and running a fund is a lot like having children. You simply cannot know what it is like to be a parent until you have kids. You can attend parenting and childbirth classes, you can read books on raising children, and you can babysit your niece or nephew all you want. None of these things, no matter how much you do them, will allow you to truly understand what it is like to be a parent until you actually have your own kids. The same is true for running a fund. But I am getting way ahead of myself.

The manner in which an SBRE entrepreneur capitalizes his deals follows what I believe is a very predictable pattern. This pattern poses for our SBRE entrepreneur what I call the "Small Balance Real Estate Dilemma." Simply stated, the dilemma is *how to evolve and improve the ability to raise capital for whatever deals the SBRE entrepreneur is doing as the volume and size of those deals, as well as the complexity of the overall business, grows over time.* This seems like it might be easy, but it is extremely difficult beyond a certain point, a point that is usually well before the ambitious SBRE entrepreneur is satisfied in growing his business. The reasons it is difficult are not well understood by most, and how to transcend the dilemma has not been written about anywhere else that I am aware of. A big part of why I understand it so deeply is that it was *my* dilemma as an ambitious small balance real estate entrepreneur, and it is also the dilemma that all of my clients face to one degree or another, which forces them to make some important decisions along the way. Let's look at that journey.

THE PROGRESSION OF SMALL BALANCE REAL ESTATE ENTREPRENEURS

SBRE entrepreneurs come from various places. You may have worked as, or for, a mortgage broker, real estate lender, developer, builder, loan servicing shop, or attorney and/or worked in many other environments in and around the real estate business. At one point or another, you decided it was time to go out on your own and do deals. It is a cliché, but you can only do one deal at a time, and SBRE entrepreneurs often start out with just one deal. In order to fund that first deal, many will put up their own money to do it, combined with borrowing the rest as needed. You may have enough capital to do one or two or three deals, or even more, depending on the financial point from which you are starting. Quite often, however, you quickly reach the outer edge of your personal resources and must start taking in capital from others in order to do more deals. Usually this is from what I refer to as FFR (friends, family, and relatives), people who know, like, and trust you. Depending on the depth of your FFR, this can carry you a significant distance early in the life of the business and allow you to do several deals or even more.

As your business and reputation grows, often the SBRE entrepreneur has access to more and more deals that meet your criteria, which you could acquire and fund *if you just had the capital*. As more capital is tied up in existing deals that perhaps have yet to go full cycle, you may quickly reach the edge of your FFR capacity and must now go out to people you do not know as well and/or with whom you do not have the same level of inherent trust. This may require you to provide more analytics and rigor in your presentation to potential investors, as they want to better understand the strengths and weaknesses, the potential risks and rewards of the deal, and generally this is something most SBRE entrepreneurs can figure out how to do reasonably well. After all, real estate deals is what you do, so providing some support of your recommendation to invest is relatively easy. If you are driven, ambitious, determined, and even halfway competent, gaining additional investors to do individual deals and matching those investors with those deals is not particularly difficult.

I know many SBRE entrepreneurs who have actually scaled their business quite some distance with this one-investor-one-deal-at-a-time model. If you are a good real estate underwriter and are providing solid returns, generally your investors will tell other investors they know about it, and you will be able to expand your pool of one-off investors significantly, allowing you to do more deals using this model. This seems like a good thing, and it is in some ways. It is also sowing the seeds of stagnation in the model and great difficulty later in transcending it because you are conditioning your investors on how the model works. They are quite content to pick and choose which particular deals they say yes or no to. But for now, the entrepreneur is not too concerned about this, because your business is growing. Many often just live with the annoyances of the model, which are also growing, because it is working more than it is not and you do not yet know of any better way.

As the SBRE entrepreneurial enterprise grows, your success is at the same time giving rise to a new prerequisite in your business—the obligation to accurately track, account for, and administer the financial performance of the assets and the capital accounts for your investors. In the beginning, simple tools like Excel and Quicken can handle the fairly rudimentary calculations that do not require particularly talented or specialized people to perform them. This isn't what the entrepreneur especially enjoys doing or is particularly good at, but it doesn't seem like a big deal and is more or less an afterthought at this early stage. Rarely is it an area that is carefully architected and built when the business is rather small, and therefore it often gets built on a foundation that is not designed to support the type and height of structure our entrepreneur has in his mind. You'll find much more on this in chapter 8.

As business continues to grow and deal sizes get bigger, the next step of your progression is often to place more than one investor into an individual deal. While many investors can write a check for $50,000 or $100,000 or $250,000, far fewer can or will write one for $500,000 and even fewer for $1 million or more. However, as your reputation, your business, and your ambitions grow, you may have opportunities to do deals that meet your underwriting criteria that are getting larger and larger, and it is simply harder to find investors with deep enough pockets to invest $1 million or more in one deal. The first, most obvious, least difficult, and least regulatory burdensome option to do these deals is to combine two or more investors together into a single deal and provide each with a fractional or participation interest in that deal prorated to their level of investment.

While there are more moving parts to this structure and potential legal and regulatory requirements—depending on the type of deal, the state that one is operating in, the residency of the investors, and other factors—it is still not particularly difficult to arrange and close deals using this method. Part of why this is relatively easy to effectuate is that the investors still have the ability to say yes or no to each deal they look at and thus have veto power over their participation in any given deal. The impact on capital-raising of this ability to pick and choose is critical to understand, and its importance cannot be overestimated, as we discuss later. For now, at this stage of the progression, the SBRE entrepreneur has figured out how you can raise greater dollar amounts in each deal and thus do more and larger deals. This development also significantly increases the annoyance factor to the entrepreneur, since you have to deal with multiple investors for each deal. The logistical and operational challenges are exacerbated as the number of investors per deal grows. You now find yourself, for example:

- providing the same deal information to multiple people
- answering the same questions and handling the same objections from more people
- trying to get multiple decisions to participate or not
- chasing them all down for their committed funds in time to close,
- replacing last-minute fallouts while holding your counterparty (borrower, seller, etc.) at bay
- and many more

To further complicate your life, you now have significantly increased the intricacy of details necessary to accurately track, account for, and administer each deal with multiple investors in them, not usually your favorite thing to do or to manage. This area of your business quickly becomes more complex and demanding of your time and brainpower to develop.

Often your success now attracts more deals and more investors who want in on the action in the structure you have created. Momentum carries you further downstream toward the rapids, and you close more and more deals using this structure, making good money in the process but aggravating you ever more due to the inefficiencies and difficulties of the business model derived from the unwieldy capital structure you have given birth to. You start to think, or start to think more frequently, that there has to be a better way to do all this that does not require so much brain damage to get deals closed, so much work on each transaction in dealing with multiple parties, each with a different combination of people, and so much convoluted tracking on the back end. You start to think about a pooled investment fund.

The Next Step—A Blind Pool Fund

At some point along the SBRE entrepreneurial journey, most of us learn of the concept of a pooled investment fund, also commonly referred to as a "blind pool" fund or other similar names. There are different types of pooled investment funds, the most common of which is a 506 Regulation D private securities offering exempt from registration with the SEC, which is what I refer to throughout this narrative.

It seems sexy, the idea of being able to make our own decisions without having to get investor approval for every deal (often multiple approvals), and it is aspirational. But it is also scary. It is going out into a forest into which you have never ventured, and you are not really sure what is lurking out there. You've heard many stories— some good and some bad—about what it is like out there, but it is a big step, a big change, and generally speaking, inertia keeps many from doing it for some period of time, often a very long period of time. As volume keeps growing along with the increasingly complicated portfolio you have to manage, frustration at the inefficiencies of your current model mount until you reach the point where you simply feel you must try it. So you do.

This is a critical juncture in the life of the SBRE entrepreneur. Sometimes people make the transition fully, sometimes partially, and sometimes it proves to be a complete waste of time and money. There are many factors that go into whether or not this transition goes smoothly or bumpily and whether it ever really succeeds or not. These factors largely determine whether or not capital can and will be raised in the fund, and they are the topics I focus on for the remainder of this book. For now, the point to be made is that a pooled investment fund is often perceived by the SBRE entrepreneur as *the answer and the solution* to the dilemma of how to have all the capital you need to be able to handle your potential deal volume. The reality is that it might be that for some people in some situations, but it is *not* in and of itself a panacea. There are many aspects to creating, launching, and running a fund successfully that must be addressed, and those who go into it with a mind-set that it is going to require commitment, perseverance, and continual learning and improvement are far more likely to succeed than those who view it as a cure-all to their capital-raising challenges. Even though there are much greater efficiencies and more systemization to be gained in a pooled fund format, in many ways raising capital in a pooled fund is *more* difficult than doing it one deal at a time. It can be more difficult but also more rewarding if done well, which will be our goal to learn how to do.

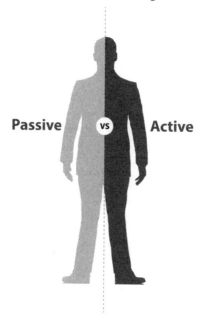

Passive vs. Active

For the SBRE entrepreneur who follows the progression above, which I consider to be fairly typical, you now come face to face with a fundamental problem you have created for yourself. You have been successful to date with the one-deal-at-a-time model (either whole or fractional interests) in which your investors can pick and choose which specific deals they want to invest in (what I call an "active" decision). This model has worked for you, and your investors are happy with it. Those investors do not have the same frustrations as you, because they are not running your business, only investing in certain deals, and so do not appreciate the reasons why you want to move to a pooled fund model. They are now being asked not to invest in an individual real estate asset-based deal you are acquiring or originating but instead to buy shares of an entity alongside an unknown number of other investors coming in at various times to invest in an unknown number of deals you will be doing at various time (what I call a "passive" decision). Even though the nature of the deals the new entity is going to invest in is the same, the fund is simply a different animal than what they have become used to that has worked so well for them. Therefore, they often resist moving to such a model where they no longer get any say in which deal is being done. The active vs. passive dynamic is huge, and its impact on capital-raising is highly underestimated by most SBRE entrepreneurs making the move to a fund.

Passive	Active
Underwrites the manager	Likes greater control
Prefers less involvement	Wants to underwrite each deal
Wants reliable income/return without asset-level decision making	Enjoys more involvement
Might have been active and reached passive stage	Prefers approving each asset-securing investment

This presents the greatest test to the willingness of the SBRE entrepreneur to transcend the one-deal-at-a-time model. You are now walking the line between doing what you have always done (and which your investors, by and large, would prefer you continue doing) and doing it in a new and uncomfortable way. It is human nature to not venture out into new and unfamiliar territory when not absolutely required to do so, even if you have heard that the temperature, terrain, and conditions are gorgeous. So generally the entrepreneur moves slowly and tentatively toward this unfamiliar territory as you try to find your footing. You try to get the fund moving, but your lack of familiarity and complete confidence with it are palpable, and you often struggle to convince investors that this new model is the way to go. It sputters and grows much more slowly than you anticipated, and you may start to justify to yourself reasons to shutter it and stick with your one-deal-at-a-time structure indefinitely. Inertia is very powerful.

"Inertia is very powerful."

This progression, or some variation of it, is, in a nutshell, the dilemma that almost all successful SBRE entrepreneurs face. I have by necessity left out many other elements of the story, such as the use of debt in financing your asset acquisitions or originations. Depending on the asset type, many SBRE entrepreneurs can borrow a big portion of the capital required to execute on your model, and this may delay or preclude your decision to investigate a pooled fund structure. By the way, SBRE entrepreneurs are very incestuous. One person's debt is another person's equity. For example, a fix-n-flipper SBRE entrepreneur may borrow 80 or 90 percent of the capital necessary to purchase a property from a hard money or private lender. The debt one gets from the other may come from a pooled investment fund run by an SBRE entrepreneur that raises the capital in the form of equity from investors even though the asset being invested into is in fact debt. If you are a flipper doing a great deal of volume, say ten houses per month, the 10 or 20 percent equity you must bring to the deals may exceed your capacity, and you may create a fund yourself from which you raise equity to bring to each deal and then borrow the rest. These kinds of inter-relationships exist everywhere in SBRE.

Drawing Some Conclusions

There are many ways to obtain the capital necessary to fund whatever types of deals an SBRE entrepreneur chooses to focus on. SBRE entrepreneurs will tend to utilize as many of these ways as possible throughout their business lifetime, and they will vary over time as the business grows or matures. They can and will obtain debt, both institutional and private. They will use private investor money as I have described above in both the one-deal-at-a-time model and in fractional or participation interests in individual deals. They may find one very large source of capital and engage in a "managed account" relationship. And they may eventually move to a pooled investment fund. I discuss each of these and others in more detail throughout the remainder of this book.

For now let me state my belief that a pooled investment fund is a logical and necessary component for most SBRE entrepreneurs who have reached a certain stage of their business. It is not easy, and it is not for everyone, to be sure, and depends on the asset model, volume, velocity, and life cycle, as well as a number of other factors. But for most, having a fund as a component of your overall program is eventually a must. It may very well be done in conjunction with one or more other capital-raising strategies and structures, but it is the pinnacle, the apex, the aspirational point of an SBRE entrepreneur's journey and provides the most reward, especially to those for whom a portion of their rewards come not just from financial compensation but also from the joy of accomplishment and mastery for their own sake. Running a fund well takes effort, commitment, discipline, and thought and should be considered a long-term proposition if it is to be done well and right.

Chapter 3

The Small Balance Real Estate Investor Continuum

The vast majority of real estate pooled investment funds that exist in the United States meet my definition of "small balance real estate funds." Yet the mainstream media and most real estate industry publications focus on large, institutional real estate market players on both sides of the equation (fund managers and investors). This is true for nearly all of the news and information I get, from virtually every source. Let me give you a great example, which I find highly typical of what I see almost everywhere.

PERPETUATING THE MYTH OF INSTITUTIONAL CAPITAL

PERE (private equity real estate) *News* is an industry news source that bills itself as follows, and this is directly from their website[1]:

---

1   www.perenews.com/Home/

"For the world's private real estate markets—PERE provides the **complete** *[emphasis mine] private real estate news and intelligence service. We cover the key players, firms, private real estate investments and deals globally. We examine the relationship between private real estate investors and private real estate fund managers. Keep your finger on the pulse of who and what is driving private real estate globally."*

Here is a summary of their weekly online news publication from December 8, 2015. The lead news story is about Blackstone holding a $15.8 billion (yes, $15,800,000,000) final close for BREPVIII. It also contains profiles of eight real estate players, including four on the deal/sponsor side and four on the investor side. On the deal side, we have Blackstone (the largest real estate private equity firm in the world), Greystone (a downtown Manhattan real estate firm with many business units, employees, and interests), Ivanhoe Cambridge (according to Wikipedia, one of the ten largest real estate companies in the world), and the Praedium Group (another downtown Manhattan real estate private equity company, with a nearly $1 billion fund).

On the investor side of the equation, we have the New York State Common Retirement Fund ($185 billion in assets, the third largest pension fund in the United States), Ohio Police and Fire Pension Fund (with a "mere" $14 billion in AUM), the South Dakota Investment Council (whose recent allocation to the Lone Star Real Estate Fund IV was $243 million on the heels of $300 million to Blackstone), and the Teacher Retirement System of Texas (another gigantic pension fund). Obviously these capital sources have significant allocations available to the real estate space, virtually none of which is available to SBRE entrepreneurs.

Now, I have nothing against this publication or any of the fund managers or investors they profile. But to say that this is the "complete" private real estate news and intelligence service is only true if one's definition of "complete" totally excludes anything that is not in the many hundreds of millions or billions of dollars. They say they "examine the relationship between private real estate investors and private real estate fund managers," but they leave out the critical words "institutional only." There is not one article or one word about any SBRE fund manager or noninstitutional investor—at least not that I was able to find—in the entire edition of their newsletter or the several others I scanned when writing this material. And this is not unique to this publication. Most of the conferences I attend, newsletters I come across, email lists I am on, and articles I see focus almost entirely on this institutional segment of the real estate market. While it might make for interesting reading, it is of virtually no direct value to the vast majority of SBRE entrepreneurs in terms of helping them deal with their day-to-day realities, challenges, and opportunities.

Unfortunately, this bias toward institutional reporting tends to distort the viewpoint of many new SBRE fund managers and helps foster widespread misunderstanding among them about what works and what doesn't in the SBRE fund space when it comes to raising capital. I am continually amazed at the number of SBRE fund managers who think that merely by the act of creating and launching a pooled investment fund they are somehow going to be able to attract institutional capital. For a lot of reasons that I will touch upon, obtaining institutional capital, *especially* in the form of an investment in shares of an SBRE fund, is extremely difficult and statistically highly unlikely for the vast majority of SBRE fund managers. The statistical reality does not, however, prevent many of them from trying. The good news is that there are other sources of capital that are a far better fit for SBRE funds, and we discuss how to tap into these more successfully.

"Obtaining institutional capital, especially in the form of an investment in shares of an SBRE fund, is extremely difficult and statistically highly unlikely for the vast majority of SBRE fund managers."

THE REAL SOURCE OF SBRE INVESTMENT CAPITAL

Having launched and run seven SBRE funds with Fairway over the years, and having now helped to architect, structure, and create more than a hundred more for various clients over the past four years, I have the luxury of both direct experience in, and first-hand observations of, the ways in which noninstitutional SBRE fund managers go about raising capital for their funds, both successfully and unsuccessfully, and from which sources. While no one approach necessarily works or fails to work for every SBRE fund, there absolutely are general principles at work that greatly influence success or failure in capital-raising from any given type of investor. My unfortunate experience is that most SBRE fund managers, including a younger version of myself, do not clearly understand these principles and thus waste a great deal of time pursuing low probability paths and obtain suboptimal results. It helps tremendously to create, maintain, and follow—and then to continually update, revise, and improve—a *written* capital raise strategic plan that articulates the strategy, tactics, and game plan you will follow. I describe such a written plan in much more detail in chapter 6.

For now, it will benefit your understanding of our discussion to recognize what I call the "SBRE Investor Continuum" and to begin to learn and accept how it works. Essentially, the continuum describes the universe of potential investor groups that you as an SBRE entrepreneur may target to raise capital for your fund. I have arranged this list more or less in order from the smallest and least sophisticated to the largest and most institutional in nature. This list is not in perfect order, as there is no perfect order, and there is some overlap from one to another in some cases. It does, however, more or less represent the world of potential investors who can theoretically capitalize your pooled investment fund and/or syndications for that matter. It should be noted and reinforced here that there are major differences in raising capital for SBRE blind pool funds vs. individual syndications, including the general bias and level of interest from each of the below investor groups toward one structure or the other, and that my discussion unless otherwise noted is focused on raising capital for SBRE blind pool funds.

The continuum of investors looks something like this:
- unaccredited investors
- accredited high-net worth (HNW) investors
- ultra-high-net worth (UHNW) investors
- registered investment advisors/wealth managers (RIA)
- single-family offices (SFO)
- multi family offices (MFO)
- broker-dealers (BD)
- foundations
- endowments
- hedge funds / private equity
- pension funds

On the one end of the spectrum, we begin with the easiest and most common source of capital for SBRE entrepreneurs, the low-hanging fruit. When first starting your SBRE enterprise, if you are like many SBRE entrepreneurs, you seek and accept capital from whomever is in your immediate network, which often consists of relatively small, mostly unaccredited investors. When matching them up with one-deal-at-a-time, this is generally not a problem from a legal standpoint and is quite common.[2] Many first-time SBRE fund managers who are making the leap to a pooled investment fund from your one-deal-one-investor-at-a-time or fractional/syndication model typically already have a base of investors that are a combination of unaccredited and accredited HNW investors, and you will often want to continue to be able to accept capital from your unaccredited investors.

There are a number of important issues to consider around accepting unaccredited investors in a 506 Regulation D fund, and I highly encourage managers to engage competent legal counsel to advise on what can and cannot be done in this regard. In my opinion, the unaccredited investor does not represent a good long-term solution to the capital-raising challenges of the SBRE fund manager and should be avoided in a pooled fund format from the beginning. I have already stated my opinion that institutional capital is also a very bad fit and largely a waste of time to pursue. So if the top and the bottom of the continuum should be avoided, where does the smart SBRE fund manager focus his or her efforts? The answer lies in the middle.

---

2   Please see my "Word of Caution" on page 7.

WHERE TO FOCUS ON THE CONTINUUM

The SBRE industry is marked by a lack of thorough statistics and data about SBRE funds, both on the investor side and the deal side. The fragmentation of the market and the private nature of 506 Regulation D funds makes it difficult to obtain accurate information about the breakdown of investors in such funds and thus much data is anecdotal. Given the nature of our business at Fairway and the number of SBRE managers we work with around the country, I believe we have as good and comprehensive anecdotal data as anyone. My goal in this chapter is to leverage this experience to help you invest your time as wisely as possible in your capital-raising efforts and focus on areas with the highest probability of return on your investment of time.

In my experience and opinion, the highest likelihood of obtaining reliable capital comes from HNW investors, UHNW investors, RIAs, and, with a higher degree of difficulty in gaining traction, family offices, with the first two representing the backbone of the investor base. Let's focus briefly on each of them in turn to paint a clearer picture of precisely what these targets look like.

Accredited High-Net Worth (HNW) Investors

By far the most widespread category of investor in SBRE funds are accredited HNW investors, but they are in fact not a large percentage of the population. The Securities Exchange Commission defines what it means to be an "accredited investor." Although the definition changes from time to time and can be somewhat complex, the most common ways an individual will be considered an accredited investor under the SEC's current rules are to have a net worth of at least $1 million, excluding the value of one's primary residence, or to have income of at least $200,000 each of the past two years (or $300,000 combined with one's spouse if married), with a reasonable expectation of making at least this amount in the current year. (See https://www.investor.gov/news-alerts/investor-bulletins/investor-bulletin-accredited-investors for more information.) Most estimates reflect that about 3 to 4 percent of American households are categorized as accredited.

My general definition of HNW for the purposes of our capital-raising efforts would be those investors in the range of $1 million to $10 million in net worth. These people represent the most reliable, if quite fragmented, source of capital for SBRE fund managers and will typically invest in the $50,000 to $250,000 range and perhaps sometimes more if they are more familiar with real estate investing. A significant effort should be made when considering an overall marketing strategy and supporting tactics toward catering to the needs of this group.

Ultra-High-Net Worth (UHNW) Investors

These people are also accredited investors but possess a much larger net worth and more investing horsepower than the ordinary HNW investor. For our purposes, I would define the UHNW investor as someone with a net worth of $10M to $50M or thereabouts. I could not find reliable data about the percentage of households meeting this definition, but clearly they are fewer and farther between than HNWs. My best estimate is that the figure is well less than 1 percent. While they are rarer, they can be identifiable and thus pursued systematically.

I greatly prefer first generation wealth than inherited wealth when working with UHNW investors. Often these people are entrepreneurs themselves who have exited or executives who have reached the point of significant wealth and now are looking to wisely invest it rather than work at the same pace and intensity they had to do to earn it in the first place. I believe this is an excellent source of capital for SBRE entrepreneurs for many reasons, including:

- more capital/capacity than ordinary HNW investors
- quicker decisions than more institutional investors
- better networks of other UHNW investors to leverage
- often a visceral identification with the challenges, opportunities, and plight of a younger SBRE entrepreneur
- and more.

This is a significant area of focus of Fairway's latest capital-raising efforts, and I suggest that you consider it as well.

Registered Investment Advisors (RIAs)

RIAs are essentially just aggregation points for obtaining capital from the same HNW and UHNW individuals listed above. In theory, working with the RIA allows the SBRE entrepreneur the ability to access many HNW and/or UHNW investors at once if he can get the RIA to recommend and place his clients' capital with him. This is true to some degree but comes with a great deal of considerations that have nothing to do with whether or not the SBRE fund being discussed is a good investment or not. Any time you are attempting to get a third party to do something, you must understand the issues and motives impacting and influencing that party. These issues and motives are generally not at all obvious and may be completely divorced from the viability of the investment for their clients, who, if you were able to get to them directly, might be very interested in and happy with the investment opportunity.

We have had some success in this realm, as have some other SBRE entrepreneurs I advise, coach, and work with, and it is definitely a viable channel. It is also a dangerous one in terms of potentially absorbing huge amounts of time trying to figure out which ones to approach and how to approach them, attempting to deal with their due diligence processes, and other often time-wasting actions that end up with nothing to show for them. It also has the possible downside of concentration risk, meaning that if you are successful in getting the RIA to place many of their clients' money with you, you expose *all* of that capital to the risk of flight if that RIA changes his or her mind later about that recommendation. This can and does happen frequently in that world, again due to other considerations.

	Pros	Cons
HNW	direct relationship with individuals make quicker decisions most prevalent source relatively easy to locate	may require more hand holding more investors to track relatively small dollar amounts
UHNW	large investment capacity often very entrepreneurial minded easier to relate than institutional	hard to get an audience with demand more terms than HNW investors
RIA	provide exposure to HNW and UHNW investors significant investment capacity	motives and operational realities misaligned potential to divest entire investment
FO	greateset SBRE investment capacity can provide SBRE managers access to entire investor continuum	difficult to penetrate intitutional-level due-diligence requirements

Family Offices

A significantly more difficult group to penetrate, but potentially well worth the effort, are family offices. There is no hard and fast definition of "family office"—no clear demarcation line between the UHNW investor and a small family office. Some UHNW investors would in fact consider themselves a single-family office. The term "family office" most often refers to a single-family office (SFO), which is a private company that manages investments and trusts for a single, very wealthy family. The company's financial capital being managed is that family's own wealth, sometimes accumulated over multiple generations.

Sometimes a family member, perhaps even the patriarch or an offspring, is actively involved. Many times, however, they are not, and therefore you (the SBRE entrepreneur) are dealing with an employee of the people who actually own and control the wealth. I find this considerably more difficult than dealing directly with an UHNW individual who was responsible for the creation of their own wealth and now is tasked with investing it. However, family offices control a great deal of wealth and thus cannot be ignored as a possible source of capital for the SBRE entrepreneur. While not as unlikely as institutional capital, the success rate of obtaining capital from family offices is considerably lower than from HNW investors, UHNW investors, and RIAs.

Multi family offices (MFOs) are even more difficult. An MFO is a family office that serves multiple families and in many ways resembles a large RIA firm, albeit with a broader scope of services than just investment advice and management. I will not spend much time on it here, as I believe it begins to approach institutional capital in its approach to investing and thus becomes a much less probable source of capital for most SBRE entrepreneurs. In short, if you are going to go after family offices, SFOs are a more likely source than MFOs.

FINAL THOUGHTS

Each of the different investor types on the continuum have different characteristics, different likes and dislikes, and different forces influencing their investment process, their behavior, and their decision making. Understanding what these are for each and how they differ is critical to better success and less wasted time for the SBRE entrepreneur attempting to raise capital from any of them. Some have much more similarity and overlap than others. The wider variety of types one attempts to target, the higher likelihood that their needs and decision-making processes will be completely different and thus the less chance our SBRE entrepreneur will be able to effectively create coherent strategies, approaches, and materials that will appeal to each. Again, this does not prevent many from trying, even though statistically it is virtually impossible they will meet with success across the whole continuum (especially the further they delve into the institutional side of the equation).

Though the investor types have widely different characteristics—varying greatly even within each type—there are ways to develop strategies to focus on particular types in the continuum. Managers with higher AUM, deeper experience, and larger teams and resources will typically have a better chance of obtaining institutional capital. New managers with little or no AUM will almost never do it and are far better off focusing on the handful of categories I detail here, particularly the HNW and UHNW investors. By simply understanding and accepting that there is a continuum, that each type of investor along the continuum has its own characteristics, and that some are far more likely to be receptive and successful for SBRE funds than others, the SBRE entrepreneur can begin to formulate a more intelligent approach to raising capital. The statistics around where the capital is most likely to come from, however difficult to obtain and however anecdotal they are, do not lie, and managers seeking to spend their time and their capital-raising budget wisely should focus on those with the highest probability of success.

Chapter 4

Small Balance Real Estate Funds–Structure Matters

Perhaps the most widespread problem that impairs raising capital in a pooled investment fund is poor, mismatched, unattractive, or simply wrong fund structure. It is frankly an epidemic in small balance real estate funds and is even more prevalent with first-time managers. There are many reasons why it is so important to nail the structure that will increase the chances of raising capital successfully—from aligning the interests of the investors with those of the manager, to properly allocating the revenue streams to the costs necessarily incurred to generate those revenue streams, to allowing the fund activities and results to be appropriately tracked and administered. Most are widely misunderstood and/or neglected, to the great detriment of both managers and investors. It is a vast topic, and here I focus on what I believe are the most important elements to the SBRE entrepreneur when creating and running your pooled investment fund.

WHAT IS "STRUCTURE"?

The very concept of fund structure is foreign to most new managers because they usually have not ever had to consider it when working in the one-deal-at-a-time or fractional/syndication model. In using the term "structure" I am referring to the myriad interrelated business, economic, administrative, and practical elements of the offering which will immediately and continuously come into play for the fund manager. The economic and business structure will have far more impact on your ultimate success or failure running a fund than the legal component, assuming you have competent counsel and assuming you run the fund with integrity and good judgement. Good structure helps attract investors, provides necessary and appropriate compensation to the manager for the work performed, can be more easily and accurately tracked and administered, and balances the realities you will face as a manager on multiple fronts with the needs and desires of your investors. Good structure is the foundation of a fund that stands a good chance of success rather than one that is doomed before it even launches.

SBRE entrepreneurs tend to rely solely on legal counsel when creating a fund to determine what structure their fund will possess, which is a grave mistake. The legal element is of course a very important component of creating a fund but it is only one component. Counsel's role is to create a set of offering documents that comply with securities law and which help to protect their client from the numerous risks of what is essentially a private offering of securities. This is what they are good at and view as their primary objective when engaged to "create a fund" for clients. But compliance with securities law in your offering documents and adhering to the many rules, regulations, and require-ments of operating such a pooled investment fund is not what I mean by structure. This is rather simply "table stakes." They are the price of entry into the game and are the rubrics by which the game must be played. But this is not structure.

Let me start with some questions you will want to ask yourself that will begin to address multiple elements of structure. These questions and many others are very important to ask, and it's also important to understand the considerations and implications behind any answers or choices you might make when you are creating a pooled investment fund. The answers to these questions are at the core of the work I do when helping clients set up a fund that will give them the best chance of success in raising capital, and they are an excellent place for you to start.

> *"These questions and many others are very important to ask, and it's also important to understand the considerations and implications behind any answers or choices you might make when you are creating a pooled investment fund."*

- What is my investment strategy for the fund?
  - That is, what kind of deals am I going to do inside of the fund and how broad or narrow should that investment strategy be?
  - What impact does this decision have on my ability to raise capital, on my ability to value the assets for the purposes of share price calculation, on real estate market gyrations and cycles, and other factors?
- How much capital am I going to need to raise and over what time period?

- Should my fund be open ended or closed ended? Why?
- Who is my ideal investor target audience?
- Is the fund going to be structured as debt or equity (or both)?
  - That is, am I going to borrow money from investors, or am I going to sell them shares of the fund entity?
  - What impact does this decision have on when and how I have to pay investors back, on accepting self-directed IRA capital, on when and how I accept and deploy capital, and on myriad other factors?
- Am I going to use leverage for the fund or the assets in it?
  - Will that be for each asset or for the fund as a whole?
  - If so, how much? Should I place limitations on it?
  - How does this impact my investors' decisions to invest or not?
- What sort of lock-up period should I use, and how/when will I redeem investors?
- How will I calculate the price of a share of my fund (and who is going to do that)?
- What sort of fees are appropriate?
- Which fees should go to the manager and which should go to the fund? Why?
- What sort of returns to investors do I expect to produce? How do I know?
- How much money can I expect to make as a manager at various volume levels?
- Can and/or should I allow the fund to do business with affiliated companies (those over which I have complete or partial control)?
  - If so, what parameters and limitations should I place around this type of business?

- □ What implications will this be likely to have on my ability to raise capital?
- How much of my own capital (if any) is necessary for me to invest in the fund alongside my other investors? That is, how much skin in the game is appropriate?
- What should my management team look like, and what roles/ responsibilities will be necessary?
- How do all of these decisions (and many others) interplay with one another?

As you begin to see from this list of questions, there are many important decisions to be made that will affect the performance of the fund from the very beginning. Some decisions will have immediate consequences (as in the fund manager's ability to raise capital), and some will only come into play over time as the fund gets off the ground and matures. Different decisions will have different implications at different points in time. It is very helpful to have appropriate guidance throughout this process whenever possible, and relevant guidance can be very difficult to come by. There are a lot of people from whom new managers will seek advice who really do not possess the slightest idea or experience with the myriad ramifications to the SBRE entrepreneur of any particular advice they may espouse. Their advice is generally far more likely to be borne from their own experiences and perspectives, which many times are totally irrelevant and unsuited to SBRE funds, as in the case of institutional fund managers, who face completely different circumstances. In my line of work, I see a lot of advice being given to fund managers that may be perfectly relevant to some other situation but that will not work, or be at all likely to work, for them. Let's discuss some of the most important issues.

FEES, COMPENSATION, AND ALIGNMENT OF INTERESTS

Probably no other topic is more near and dear to the hearts of both managers and investors than money and how and when it gets split up and distributed. Depending on the asset model and the nature of the fees being charged, there are many ways to structure the collection and allocation of those fees. For the purposes of this discussion, let's picture a continuum of possibilities ranging from highly investor friendly (or "aligned") to highly manager focused (or "not aligned"). I have seen both ends of the spectrum and have worked with new managers who have structured their fund at either end of that spectrum, as well as many who settle somewhere in the middle. The primary issue here is the balance between making the fund attractive to investors and helping to remove barriers to raising capital on the one hand and creating a fee structure that doesn't starve the manager and preclude him from allowing the fund to get off the ground in the first place on the other. The early days of running a fund are often the hardest for many reasons, not the least of which is that it is difficult for the manager to earn enough income to reach critical mass if the fund has been structured with complete investor alignment in mind.

The example of a mortgage pool fund (a fund whose asset strategy is to make real estate secured loans—typically hard money, bridge, or construction loans) is a great way to illustrate the issue. Typically these loans carry interest rates that range from 10 percent on the low side (maybe lower if our fund manager is lending in the state of California, which has the lowest interest rates anywhere in the country for hard money loans) to 15 percent and sometimes more, as well as loan fees, also called points, in the range of 2 to 6 percent of the loan amount. Let's say that the fund manager is charging an average of

12 percent interest and 4 points. Let's also say that these are bridge/construction loans whose average duration are six months, meaning the capital can be turned over twice per year, so there are a total of 8 points (8 percent) paid in loan fees on that same capital. How, when, and to whom these fees are allocated makes a huge difference. Here is how and why.

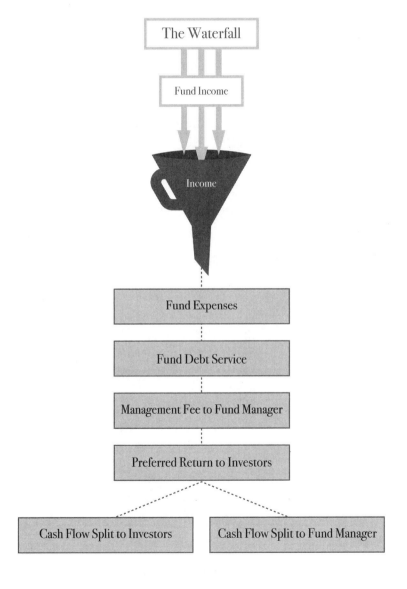

The most aligned structure would have all of the income, both interest and points, coming into the fund itself, running through the priority of cash flows (often called the "Waterfall"), and only after a certain level of performance to the investor (either a preferred return or a hurdle) would any remaining profit or excess distributable cash be split between the investors and the manager. The least aligned structure would have the manager keeping *all* of the points for himself, not running them through the fund, and only paying the investors the interest income (less some amount for fund-related expenses and other fees). The former aligns the interests of the investors and the manager far more because now it does not matter whether the deal is priced at 12 percent and 4 points or 10 percent and 6 points or any other combination of rate and fees that may be actually neutral to the borrower. The result to the fund and the investors will be the same. The latter structure incentivizes the manager to charge higher fees (since he is keeping them) and, if necessary to get the deal from the borrower vis-à-vis whatever competition exists for that loan, lower the interest rate.

Many managers say, "I would never do that," and I believe most of them are sincere going in. But the fact is that a structure whereby the manager is keeping all the fees can create behaviors and actions that are not necessarily in the interests of the investor. Since the investor in a blind pool is completely abdicating asset level decision making to the manager and has no control at all about which deals get done, when, and at what pricing, it is much easier for that investor to make the decision to invest if the inherent fee structure of the fund does not allow for manager manipulation to his own benefit. The flip side to this is that many managers *need* the income from the points and in most cases have become used to receiving all or most of them in the one-deal-at-a-time model, in order to pay the bills and keep the lights on. If they no longer keep these fees and instead throw them into the fund as income and only get paid if/when all fund expenses have been covered and the investors have received a preferred return, it can take a significant period of time for them to earn the same level of income they were earning in the one-deal-at-a-time or fractional model. They can and should once the AUM has grown to a size sufficient to produce attractive returns, subject to performance of the fund, but they cannot earn a lot of money by just churning deals and keeping the points, potentially at the expense of their investors, if the structure is fully aligned.

There are many other situations and examples of how fees can be charged inside a pooled investment fund that are somewhere on the continuum of alignment. I do not have the space here to articulate them all, but I do want to conclude this section of our discussion with my overarching belief on this topic, which is this: In all such cases, there should be some intelligent balance between aligning the interests of the investor with those of the manager and at the same time compensating the manager sufficiently to cover the costs associated with providing whatever services are needed to make the fund a reality and to produce a return to those investors. "Put the money where the work is" is a saying I use a lot when advising clients in the structure and setup of their fund. The key is that the fees and compensation should be sufficient to cover costs and offset actual overhead but not to generate large profits for the manager regardless of fund performance. The real profitability to the manager should only come, ideally, after expenses have been paid and the investors have received a preferred return (and, in the case of certain types of asset models and specifically with closed-ended funds, a return of their full capital account). Fees being paid to the manager along the way should not be excessive but rather sufficient to cover actual costs necessary to operate the fund in the first place. The real juice in the fund should come after investors have been rewarded as well.

"There should be some intelligent balance between aligning the interests of the investor with those of the manager and at the same time compensating the manager sufficiently to cover the costs associated with providing whatever services are needed to make the fund a reality and to produce a return to those investors."

DEFINING THE INVESTMENT MANDATE

Another major consideration when setting up the fund is determining the nature, scope, and breadth of the types of assets and investments that are to be pursued by the manager on behalf of the investors. It really comes down to how broad or narrow the mandate should actually be, and there are different schools of thought on this topic. On the one hand, savvy investors want to have some specific parameters around the types of deals the manager is able to do so that they have some clear scope of what business the fund is in. I have seen funds that literally were allowed to do any type of investment imaginable—real estate, oil and gas, coins, operating businesses, car loans, etc. This type of mandate is, in my judgment, way too broad.

On the other hand, being simply a one-trick pony can be very dangerous. Real estate markets cycle, and not every strategy works all of the time. Depending on whether the fund is open or closed ended and other factors, there can be real value to both the manager and the investors in allowing the fund some flexibility to pursue different strategies during different market cycles. This is easier said than done, as the manager should possess the requisite expertise to underwrite any deal types that are included in the strategy and should also have enough of a platform to originate or acquire whatever asset types are included in the mandate. Finding the balance between keeping the mandate narrow enough so that the manager cannot do literally anything and keeping it broad enough so as to not become completely stuck in a changing market cycle, and doing it in a way that will appeal to investors, is more art than science. It pays to make the decision thoughtfully at the outset of the fund.

TO LEVERAGE OR NOT TO LEVERAGE?

The decision to use debt or not, how much, what form, and when is extremely important and influential on multiple levels. Debt can be very dangerous, as I experienced up close and personal with our large credit facility that did not renew (see the introduction). It can also be extremely helpful to improving returns to shareholders. It can help you better manage cash flows in and out of the fund, improving the timing and acceptance of investor capital and minimizing the drag on fund yields that sitting on too much cash can produce. It can be simultaneously valuable and precarious.

Not all debt is created equal. There is a big difference between using more permanent leverage to grow the AUM and simply using warehouse lines to help with the timing of closing deals and managing cash. There is a big difference between fund-level credit facilities and asset-level, non-comingled debt. There is a big difference between placing a huge reliance on a single source of debt with covenants, eligibility requirements, and restricted accounts attached and utilizing debt from multiple sources and spreading out the risk.

Many fund managers and investors alike have visceral reactions to the use of leverage and are either afraid of it or in love with it, both often to their own detriment. To my mind, using debt intelligently and wisely is an important tool in the fund manager's arsenal. The challenge is that many do not understand how to use it well, where and when it is available, what true strings are attached to it, and how to match the nature of the underlying assets and the overall structure of the fund to the type, level, and amount of debt they actually use. Like many other aspects of structure, there is no one universal right or wrong approach. It must be well considered and thoughtfully approached.

DOING BUSINESS WITH AFFILIATES

Another critical decision involves the degree to which the fund is going to be allowed to do business (and consequently have financial interactions) with other entities that are owned or controlled by the manager of that fund. It is highly common that the manager already has an operating business before launching the fund—a mortgage origination company, a real estate brokerage, a property management firm, or some other real estate oriented enterprise. This entity will often be relied upon to provide services to the fund in the form of asset origination, brokerage, property management, title work, or other such services. Is the fund going to hire these entities to perform this work? If so, how and when will these entities be compensated? How will that compensation be determined? Will the fund provide capital to any of the entities to acquire assets? If so, under what terms will this capital be provided? Since the manager controls the decisions for both the fund and the other entity, what is to prevent him from favoring the entity from which he stands to gain more money more quickly?

This is a very delicate topic, and it comes up virtually every time I am engaged to help SBRE entrepreneur clients set up their fund. Fundamentally it is perfectly legal to do all of this, although there are certain legal issues that must be addressed and followed regarding proper disclosure to investors, and this is a good example of an issue that you will want to discuss carefully with your attorney. From a capital-raising standpoint, it comes down to alignment or lack thereof and conflicts of interest, real or perceived, and the impact that allowing the fund to engage in these affiliated transactions has on investors' willingness to invest or not. Some amount of related party transactions are just about universal in SBRE funds. The degree, scope, boundaries, and limitations that managers are willing to put on these affiliate transactions vary widely and influence to one degree or another, varying by manager and circumstances, the attractiveness of the offering to the investors.

FUND GOVERNANCE AND TRANSPARENCY

As I discuss in chapter 2, investors are leery of "blind pool funds" because they lose any ability to pick and choose the individual deals. In fact, they are abdicating complete responsibility to the manager for not only those investment decisions but for every other aspect of running that fund. This level of autonomy in decision making and operational independence necessarily restricts the amount of control investors have and places them in a position of vulnerability to less competent, trustworthy, or diligent managers. Rightly, investors are more cautious and suspecting when investing in blind pools than one-off deals that they can review and decide upon, not to mention perfect a security interest in. There are quite simply many things the manager can do behind the scenes that the investor will be highly unlikely to ever even know about until it is way too late.

In addition to aligned fund structure in the first place, the only other real way to help ameliorate these concerns is to provide strong fund governance and transparency to the fund investors. There is once again a spectrum of possibilities ranging from hardly any to many things the manager can do to implement good governance and transparency. I discuss this in more depth in chapter 8, but here are some of the simplest and most common ways to do this:

- Hire a third party fund administration company. There are many good ones, and this is an easy way for the manager to give additional confidence to investors that the fund is being administered professionally and responsibly.
- Have the fund financial statements audited annually. This is probably the best way for investors to get some verification of the financials and the assets.
- Create an advisory board (most often nonfiduciary) and include some of your early or largest investors on that board.
- Provide regular communication to investors about ongoing developments in the fund. I suggest quarterly as the best rhythm that is frequent enough but not overly burdensome to the manager to produce. Provide both quantitative and qualitative information and commentary, and be open and forthcoming on what is happening, both positive and negative.
- Develop written policies and procedures for how you do things, and review them with counsel. Possibilities include an investment committee to make asset decisions, underwriting criteria, disaster recovering plans, key person policies and

procedures, life insurance on key persons, orderly liquidation policies, and more.

- Utilize an investor portal to provide important information to investors and give them password-protected access. You can utilize this portal to regularly update financials, quarterly reports, asset level information, and more.

Some or all of these things can be baked into the fund's offering documents and committed to by the manager before launching. Different managers will be able to commit to differing levels of these policies depending on where they are in the maturity of their businesses. Even if you cannot do all of them, a few are better than none at all. Since investors are being asked to place their trust in someone and something over which they have little to no control, incorporating some basic governance and transparency policies into the fund up front goes a long way toward inspiring that trust.

FINAL THOUGHTS

One thing I know for certain—you cannot please all of the people all of the time. This is very true when setting up a fund as well. No matter what structure you come up with, there will be some people who do not like that structure and who will tell you that you should have done this or that differently. Many times they may be absolutely right if the fund has been set up without consideration given to the needs of your investors. This is why it is so important to understand who your most likely target audience of investors is in the first place, which is almost never institutional investors in the case of SBRE funds. Often, however, people do not really understand all of the considerations that should go into the creation of an SBRE fund, including your investors, attorneys, CPAs, and other counterparties you are likely to consult with if considering taking this step. Their opinions and/or desires are often based on a single angle or viewpoint that does not comprehend the totality of interrelated factors you are going to encounter if you do decide to launch and run a fund.

It is very hard for most SBRE entrepreneurs to grasp how things will actually work once a pooled investment fund capital structure has been wrapped around your asset model. Each deal no longer stands on its own but is now comingled with all of the other deals in the fund, which requires much more sophisticated and complex tracking, accounting, and cash management than when each deal is treated in insular fashion. Multiple additional factors must now be considered when making decisions, factors that you as an SBRE entrepreneur have never had to incorporate into your asset-level decision making before and therefore do not well understand in the early stages of your new fund. The transition to having to incorporate these multiple additional factors into your decision making in order to influence fund performance is very difficult for many managers to make. You can only truly learn and absorb this lesson deeply once you have spent time managing this pooled investment vehicle, as only then do the implications of the structure become real. Most of the time, any shortcomings in structure are only discovered by default after the fact rather than being deliberately designed into the fabric of the fund. If you can, having good structure going in whenever possible, recognizing that no matter what not everyone is going to like it, makes the chances of success far greater.

Readers who want more information on this subject should go to www.SBREfunds.com/capitalflow.

Chapter 5

Disciplined Underwriting— The Holy Grail of SBRE Fund Performance

The definition of an SBRE entrepreneur necessarily requires that you are doing deals with other people's capital. There comes a time in the life of every SBRE entrepreneur when you discover that you may be able to do a deal with someone else's money that isn't a very good one for no other reason than you stand to make immediate money by doing it. Even when the investor is reviewing and approving each deal, as in the one-deal-at-a-time or fractional models, they often will have less information than you, be otherwise distracted, and/ or place significant trust and influence in your hands about when and whether to do a given deal as well as to determine the terms and conditions of that deal. As awareness of this dynamic grows, you face a moral and ethical choice about how you will handle this responsibility and stewardship of other people's money. This goes to the very core of successful SBRE entrepreneurship.

Throughout my career, I have learned two lessons over and over again. One is that capital is almost always available for genuinely good deals (and is also often available for bad ones). The second is that there are those who will exploit this fact to their own advantage, to varying degrees of egregiousness, and there are those who will treat other people's money as if it were their own. Often those in the former category will begin tepidly and only become more brazen as necessity (meaning their own financial necessity) dictates. The longer they can figure out how to make money off other people's money without losing access to that money, the better. Those in the latter category typically have longer time horizons by which they measure their success and are fewer in number. There are times when these people will be overly conservative and miss out on deals that might have performed perfectly well and enhanced yields to investors, not to mention put more money in their own pockets. But overall they are people with whom it is easier to sleep at night because they genuinely care about their investor's money, in many cases almost even more than if it were their own.

Part of the challenge from the investor perspective is that it can be very difficult to tell the two breeds apart for a long, long time—often until it is too late. To be a good underwriter of deals—a disciplined, honest, thorough, and competent underwriter—is not easy nor is it universal. Because real estate tends to move in cycles, often rather long cycles, it is relatively easy to appear to be a good underwriter when the market is only moving in a continuous upward direction. But often the real outcome of a deal is not experienced for months or even years. This is even more true and the effect more pronounced in a pooled investment fund, where the individual performance of several or many assets that are comingled together combine to determine the overall performance to investors in that fund. Exacerbating the challenge in a pooled investment fund is the fact that there is no longer any involvement from the investors in the decision-making process of each asset. Whereas in the one-deal-at-a-time or fractional/syndication models investors can pick and choose which deal they are willing to invest in by doing their own homework on it (the property, the borrower, the asset, the location, the economics, etc.), no such choice exists in the pooled investment fund model.

STEWARDSHIP VS. GREED

When I first got into the hard money lending business in the late 1980s, I worked for a federally chartered savings and loan. I had a boss who became a bit of a mentor to me over time as well as a sizable early investor in my first pooled investment fund and who passed away at an early age from cancer. He was a hard-ass of the old-school variety but one who truly cared about making smart deals that would perform or at least enable the company to recover all its investment via the collateral if it didn't. I recall very vividly him warning me when I started that first fund that the biggest risk would be in doing deals I shouldn't be doing just because no one else was looking. I had been doing private hard money loans for several years, working with several dozen investors who were funding them one deal at a time. I was already very conscious of the fact that my investors may or may not choose to spend the time to fully underwrite each deal and were relying heavily on my judgment, especially as their trust in me built up over time. I had made the choice early that I would always do my very best to disclose everything I knew about each deal to my investors—good or bad, positive or negative—about the property, the borrowers, and the risks as I understood them, so I thought this would not be any sort of an issue for me. In retrospect, I just couldn't appreciate at the time what he was saying, but over the years I have come to understand just how powerful that dynamic really is. Here is why.

Even if you have the right belief system and mind-set around investing other people's money, doing it in a blind pool fund is fundamentally different. You no longer have the backstop or out, real or perceived, of having your investor "sign-off" on the deal before you fund it (or before they buy it). As I discovered, different investors in the one-deal-at-a-time and fractional model have different levels of risk tolerance, return requirements, and underwriting criteria. Therefore, just because one investor might not do a given deal doesn't mean that another one wouldn't jump on it. In a fund, I no longer had the luxury of different investors for different deals, each of whom would ultimately say yes or no themselves. Now I (and my underwriting team, but really I, as the principal) was fully responsible for each decision, each deal, and each outcome, and each of them would combine to a greater or lesser degree to impact the overall performance of the fund. That high loan-to-value deal that Investor A would love but Investor B wouldn't—should I put that into the fund or not? Why? When should I and when should I not? I could make the decision that the fund was to pass and still then give it to Investor A and make some money on it (which is perfectly legal as long as your offering documents have the proper disclosures), but if I thought it was likely to perform well and add to the yield, why would I not put it into the fund? There is no perfect answer.

The point is that having the full autonomy to make the final decisions on when to do a deal and when not to is an authority and responsibility that is impossible to fully appreciate until you have been in that position. How a person will handle that responsibility goes a long ways toward defining him as a fund manager. This is partly where the fee alignment I mention in the last chapter becomes so important.

Let's say you are an SBRE entrepreneur managing a bridge lending fund and a deal comes along that appears decent at the outset. You bring it in to underwrite it and move down the road on it. As information is gathered, you determine that the loan-to-value ratio is at the very high end (or beyond) of your criteria, the property is less than stellar, and the borrower is marginal. You know in your heart that it is really not the best deal for the risk you (or rather the fund) are taking, but you also know there is no one there to question you if you choose to fund it, especially at the beginning. If it performs, which it may very well do if the market keeps doing well, no one will ever be the wiser. Only if it defaults and the fund cannot recover the invested amount will it ever be a potential problem, a situation that can feel very hypothetical and remote to you in the moment.

Depending on whether or not your structure allows you to keep the points on the deal, this may very well impact your decision. Let's say you are keeping all the points and let's say the fund has the capital at the moment to fund the deal. Let's say it is $500,000 and you have quoted (and the borrower has accepted) a 5 percent fee on the deal. Well, if you choose to close the loan, you will make $25,000 at closing. If you choose not to close it, you make *zero*. If money is tight for you at the time, no one is looking, and you can make a straight-faced argument if you had to that the deal meets the fund's criteria, which you can almost always do if you really want to, many managers in that situation will choose to fund that deal and take the calculated gamble that it will never become a problem for the fund (and ultimately your investors). If the structure dictated that all of the points were to go into the fund instead, you may or may not make that same decision. Aligned fund structure helps keep fund managers honest but also makes it harder for them to earn enough money when the fund is small to make a go of it, which is why, in addition to mere ignorance of options, many will choose less investor-aligned and more manager-friendly structures.

The point is that it is far easier for managers to let greed influence behavior, to make poor or self-interested decisions, and to get sloppy, or even deceptive, in those decisions in a pooled investment fund than in the one-deal-at-a-time model. Being a reliable and competent steward of other people's money is a heavy responsibility that some people take very seriously. Others will see the tremendous freedom you now possess as an opportunity to do marginal deals that a favorable market will cover up for a long period of time and on which you can make a lot of money in the meantime.

THE IMPACT OF COMPETITION

Lots of competition for deals also erodes underwriting standards and increases risks to investors. When markets are good and there is a lot of capital chasing deals, often the only way for the fund manager to compete to get deals is on price and terms. Advance rates or loan-to-value ratios (LTVs) increase, equity requirements decrease, and interest rates or economic terms become more competitive and attractive to borrowers, developers, rehabbers, and other parties seeking capital, and the only way to "win" deals in such an environment can be to lower underwriting standards. This strategy can actually appear to work just fine as long as markets are hot and others are jumping in to do even dumber underwriting than the last guy. However, when the music stops, someone is left without a chair, and this is when the most careless, egregious, and aggressive dealmakers get exposed. In a pooled investment fund, there can be myriad ways for the manager to attempt to downplay or even ignore poor performance for an asset or two without the investors knowing about it, on the hopes that subsequent assets will make up for that poor performance. This is a fool's game that good underwriters will avoid but which is quite common in deteriorating economic market cycles. The marginal deals that were done in good economic times come full circle and can pose serious problems in a fund when markets move in the other direction.

In addition, SBRE entrepreneurs will often gear up their staff and infrastructure as market conditions improve, more capital becomes available, and more deals are getting done. They hire more salespeople, underwriters, and other personnel, lease more office space, and increase overall expenses and overhead requirements. If and when markets cycle, there is less need for these people, space, and overhead, but many are not able or willing to adjust timely and properly and instead loosen underwriting standards to enable income to continue to come in, pushing off the consequences of bad deals until some future point that they hope and pray will never come. As markets deteriorate further, the worst of them may resort to outright fraud, misrepresentation, misappropriation of funds, and other acts that can be committed behind the scenes which are intended to prolong their income, even their existence, and delay the inevitable meltdown. Many more will not deliberately act in bad faith and/or commit outright fraud but will stretch the guidelines to the breaking point in order to attempt not to have to face unpleasant realities. Unfortunately, I am familiar with way too many funds that grew substantially in good times but could not muster the discipline necessary to adhere to strong, fundamental underwriting standards when markets were hot and ending up paying the painful consequences at some later point. It is a familiar story not only in SBRE funds but also in some public (and private) companies, government departments or municipalities, and other similar situations. Warren Buffett has written about the phenomena many times, and it is equally true in the world of SBRE funds.

MY PERSONAL EXPERIENCE IN THE IMPORTANCE OF GOOD UNDERWRITING

As I shared in the introduction, my company, Fairway America, and I went through some very difficult times during the 2008 financial crisis and the subsequent period that came to be known as the Great Recession. At the same time my business partner was battling cancer, a battle he would lose in a brief, twenty-two-month span, the biggest problem we faced was too great a reliance on a single capital source (WFCF). With the benefit of hindsight and hard-earned experience, I understand intimately the danger of the capital structure I had created for our fund (see chapter 4), which was comprised almost entirely of debt rather than equity. With a $50 million credit facility coming due, a lender who was unwilling to renew it despite perfect performance, no replacement lender available literally anywhere in the world, and the worst financial conditions since the Great Depression, I had inadvertently placed the fund in a position that threatened to wipe out all of my investors' capital.

What saved me (and them) more than anything else was the fact that I always placed great emphasis on diligent underwriting and making solid lending decisions that I felt would stand up to significant market corrections. We had largely maintained our underwriting disciplines through all the good times and never succumbed to the temptation to do marginal or bad deals just to make a lot of money. Believe me, we easily could have. Over the years there have been dozens—perhaps hundreds—of loans that we could easily have justified doing that would have earned us millions of additional dollars of revenue but that we didn't fund because we did not like the risk associated with them. We avoided these deals for the benefit of the investors in our fund at our own short-term expense. The deals we turned down nearly always got done elsewhere. These were decisions for which we did not earn any money nor get any credit for making at the time, and in fact it was quite the opposite. In many ways, besides just the money we would have made, it would have been easier to approve the loan and close it. Turning them down mostly just pissed a lot of people off who were involved in the deal. The borrower who wanted the loan, the broker who brought us the deal and wanted to earn his fee, the loan officers who worked for me and wanted their commission—they all had vested interests in closing it, not turning it down. It made it harder to get business from the broker the next time, harder to manage the loan officer, harder to get the borrower to ever come back. There were times where we would have an appraisal from a licensed appraiser, that *we* in fact ordered, that supported the value needed to make the loan, but that we didn't believe in and thus would decide to pass (or cut the loan amount back and lose the deal). This was never easy and required great discipline. I am not saying this to try to get a pat on the back. I am just saying it because this dynamic, this decision on how you will underwrite, will carry implications and foster situations and consequences on multiple levels and is a reality of an SBRE entrepreneur's existence. It affects your employees, your counterparties, your referral sources, your investors, and yourself.

When we reached the maturity of the credit line and could not get it renewed, we simply could not repay $26 million in one lump sum. At that point, we became in material default under the terms of our loan agreement with WFCF. Their default options included many things that would not be good for our investors, many of whom I had known for years and who were my highest priority at that point, such as sweeping all of our cash flow, terminating us as servicing agent on the loans, and otherwise taking very harsh and one-sided action to protect their investment. To their credit, they did not do any of those things as they might have in other circumstances, and the reason they didn't was because of the quality of our underwriting. Fortunately, we had plenty of fund-level equity (from their perspective—subordinated debt as far as the fund was concerned) behind them and substantial additional equity at the asset level beyond that, combining to make WFCF's exposure extremely low. More importantly, even at our highest levels of delinquency we still had more than 80 percent of our loans completely current on their monthly payments. This meant our cash flow was very strong and was never an issue, thus enabling us to negotiate an acceptable forbearance agreement with WFCF to buy the time we needed to systematically liquidate assets in order to repay them.

FINAL THOUGHTS

There is a great deal more to this story, but the moral of it is that the quality of the assets we had originated was very high and the performance, repayment, and recovery of those assets held up exceedingly well compared to most other funds of a similar nature during that time period. I don't love telling this story, as it is very personal and painful for me to have gone through. A lot of people in the real estate business went through tough times, and many had far worse outcomes than I did, so I don't expect any sympathy from anyone. But I tell it because I have had a large number of clients, SBRE entrepreneurs, and fund managers tell me how much they appreciate my sharing it. I hope that my experiences can help inspire and motivate people to make quality decisions, to be more thoughtful and thorough in their approach than they otherwise might, and to have the courage to work through challenging times while maintaining belief in yourself.

I also think it clearly and dramatically demonstrates the fact that I was able to survive mainly because of the disciplines I had in my underwriting decision making and taking a long-term view of asset-level performance rather than what it would immediately put into my own pocket. In retrospect, I made a big mistake in the capital structure, and I paid for it. Ironically, in just about any time period except the very one I did it in, that structure would have worked out just fine. Of the hundreds of loans we funded, there are definitely a few we made that, with the benefit of hindsight, I would like to have not done. None of those, however, were the result of us doing deals merely for the sake of earning the fees associated with them.

There are far more lessons to be learned in every deal that doesn't work out than in the ones that do, and I try to understand what those lessons are each time. At the end of the day, being disciplined and principled in our underwriting kept our asset-level performance strong, despite the horrible market conditions and the less-than-ideal capital structure, and allowed us to produce a far better outcome than most hard money funds of its era. For that, I am very proud. It is the number-one reason I was able to survive, pivot my business, and be in a position to be writing these words today. Always remember how important good deal underwriting is. Be disciplined, even when no one is looking, and be a steward of other people's money who is worthy of the trust they have placed in you. If you place this above all else, you will be successful.

"Always remember how important good deal underwriting is. Be disciplined, even when no one is looking, and be a steward of other people's money who is worthy of the trust they have placed in you."

Chapter 6

The Importance of a (Written) Capital Raise Strategic Plan

When I was about twenty-five years old, I first discovered the power of putting important things in writing. Earl Nightingale, in his classic work *Lead the Field*, was the person who turned me on to the fact that our ideas, plans, and goals are far more likely to materialize if they are consistently put down on paper (or in today's world, on your computer). He convinced me of the notion that "you become what you think about" and that since I can control my thoughts, I can control what I become. What a powerful and liberating idea this was to me, and I can look back on it now in my early fifties and recognize it as the most important turning point in my life.

Shortly thereafter I began to write down my dreams, ambitions, goals, and plans and subsequently kept journals of my thoughts, ideas, and experiences in business and life for many years afterward. I quickly discovered that Earl was right—if I determined what I wanted to achieve, wrote down those things as goals, developed plans and ideas for their attainment, wrote those down too, worked my ass off to make it happen, and then reflected upon what worked well and what didn't and repeated the process continually, the chances of my achieving the things I had set out to achieve increased exponentially. Better results and more success quickly followed. There were and are setbacks and obstacles, of course, but the process of thinking, writing, acting, and reflecting, and repeating those steps indefinitely, proved to be an excellent formula for progressively achieving goals that were important to me.

This is why it is extremely helpful for a wise fund manager to carefully consider his strategies, tactics, and goals for raising capital and to write them down. When you combine this general truism—that goals are more likely to be achieved if they are in writing—with the fact that most managers are far more predisposed toward the deal side of the business than the capital-raising side, it becomes even *more* important to develop a written plan. Undoubtedly it will require regular review and updating, but it forces you to work on this critical area of your business more consistently, thoughtfully, and repeatedly and significantly increases the chances of successfully raising capital once you have taken the initiative to start an SBRE fund.

DEVELOPING AN OVERALL STRATEGY

In chapter 3, I spent some time discussing the SBRE Investor Continuum, and I would encourage you to make sure you have that material fresh in your mind as you read the remainder of this chapter. There I made the assertion that institutional capital is a very poor fit for the vast majority of SBRE funds and that it is a waste of time for most SBRE fund managers to pursue it, at least as it pertains to getting institutional investors to invest in shares of a pooled investment fund.[3] I also made the assertion that unaccredited investors are

---

3   I would note that if any traction is to be gained by SBRE fund managers on
     the institutional front, it will almost always be in some form other than a

not a good long-term source of capital for SBRE fund managers and that HNW and UNHW investors are the primary target audience for the majority of SBRE funds, along with some other categories on occasion. If this is true, and even if it is not, where does a wise fund manager begin when it comes to deciding who to target, how to target them, when to target them, and in what combinations? I believe there are four important objectives to any good capital-raising strategy that you will want to pursue. Here they are, in the order in which you will want to follow them:

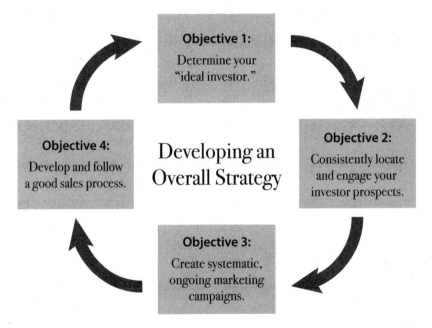

The first objective is to determine who your "ideal investor" is—not by name, but by description—and to define exactly what that is. Consider the following as specifically and in as much detail as possible:

- What characteristics does that ideal investor have?

Pari Passu LP interest in their fund. This may be a viable solution for some SBRE entrepreneurs, but it is completely different than running a discretionary fund which is the focus of this book and the focus of the type of capital raise strategic plan that I will discuss in this chapter.

- What are the demographics?
- What commonalities do they have?
- Where do they hang out?
- What do they look, sound, and feel like?

This is a very important starting point because you are going to want to try to focus your efforts *somewhere specific* as much as possible and not be trying to target everyone and do everything.[4] Not focusing your efforts is probably the most common mistake that most managers make, other than not having a written plan in the first place. Resources and time are finite and must be marshaled consciously in a particular direction for maximum results. You should do this exercise with your leadership or management team—or whatever key group you have built that will be involved in this component of your business—at the outset of your fund launch, and revisit it periodically to incorporate the lessons you will have learned from your experiences.

The second objective is to locate and consistently engage with these highest caliber investor prospects appropriate to your particular fund with a goal to create a business relationship and develop trust with them.[5] A good capital raiser will do this by developing specific strategic opportunities to meet and engage as many of his ideal investors based on some number of pillars (see below) in both group settings—conferences, events, organizations, etc.—and one-

---

4   Once you have identified your "ideal investor," be sure to talk to legal counsel about any issues you may need to address or be aware of when raising money from that kind of investor.

5   There is a major difference between a 506b and a 506c offering which allows for general solicitation and advertising of the fund and 506b which does not. The entire next chapter is devoted to a full discussion of this issue. For the purposes of the discussion in this chapter, I am assuming a 506c election by the fund manager.

on-one, typically once you have met and are cultivating longer term relationships with a subset of them. The idea here is to systematically add valuable names to your database and consistently increase the number of them every day, week, month, and year. I like to refer to this database as your metaphorical "garden" that you are tending to carefully on a daily basis. You have to make sure you have fertile soil that has been tilled and rowed, that you are planting the appropriate seeds you want to grow, that you are keeping it free of weeds, and that you fertilize and water it regularly if you ultimately want to harvest the crops at an appropriate season. You want to steadily build the amount of well-chosen plantings in your garden.

The third objective is to create systematic, ongoing marketing campaigns to deliberately and methodically inform and educate rather than "sell to" these high-value prospects. You will need to be realistic with yourself about what you are actually capable of doing given your unique skills, team resources, abilities, and so on, but you must develop some type of education-based drip marketing campaign. This is watering and fertilizing, and without it, your well-chosen seeds will not grow. You want to establish yourself as an authority on how and why to invest in the specific space your fund occupies. You should attempt to utilize a marketing approach focused on education and providing useful information to your investor prospects rather than pure advertising. The goal is to position yourself as an authoritative leader in your business space and in your targeted geographic territories, create top-of-mind-awareness (TOMA) about you and your fund, and subtly yet consistently let it be known—always within the confines of securities regulations around solicitation—that you are seeking investor money for your fund. You want people to figuratively raise their hand and say, "I'm interested."

The fourth and final component of the strategy is to put these prospective investors, those that have raised their hand and proclaimed interest, through a specific sales process designed to deepen your relationship and create trust in an orderly fashion without trying to close them too quickly. I do not like to "cold call" or "hard sell" anyone. People want to buy, not to be sold. The sales process as well as all of the other aspects of your fund should be designed to engender in them feelings of comfort and confidence in the fund's strategy and characteristics and in you as the manager. It should lead them inexorably to a yes when, and only when, the fit is right. You want to make sure that the fund is a fit for their needs and also that they are a match for yours (see the next section) before recommending an investment. The important point to understand here is that at least some sort of sales process should be considered, developed, followed, revised, and improved on an ongoing basis to improve your results. See the end of this chapter for additional thoughts about a sales process.

The order of this process does not mean that you will not proactively try to determine the best prospects, engage, and close them for an investment in your fund as quickly as is appropriate. You absolutely will. It just means that your engagement will begin by meeting them, prequalifying them, placing them in your investor "garden" first to systematically water and fertilize them, and only then put them through your sales process. You never want to convey to anyone a feeling of desperation or need on your part to have to have them as an investor, as it reduces their confidence in you. Yours will be an education-based marketing strategy to the right target audience first, followed by deeper personal engagement over time, followed by a disciplined sales process. You of course want to be able to move through the process as quickly as you can in order to raise sufficient capital to meet your asset origination or acquisition volume, but you also must recognize and accept that it *is a process*. Building the foundations of the process early and expanding, improving, and refining that process over time will greatly enhance long-term success in raising capital. Thus, balancing your short-run need to raise capital and get the fund off the ground with the long-term importance of a systematic process and approach should be a focus and a priority.

Philosophy

Another important exercise I encourage all of my clients to do early on in their fund capital-raising efforts is to develop a philosophy, or a constitution if you will, about how you will raise capital and the kinds of investors that are the best fit for you and your fund. You want to attract and accept investors that will be good to work with, fun to be around—as you will want to find ways to spend time with them—and able to help spread the word about the fund opportunity to others they know. Birds of a feather flock together, so you want to pick the right birds.

This list should really be things and ideas in which you genuinely believe rather than some list you take from me or someone else just because they may sound good. To give you an example, however, the following bullets outline some high-level thoughts, ideas, concepts, and philosophies that you might consider adopting when raising capital for your funds:

- I recognize, accept, and embrace the fact that consistent, strategic, and ongoing capital-raising is a key part of the responsibilities of a good fund manager.
- I will be truthful, honest, and transparent with all of my investors and prospects at all times.
- I will attempt to the best of my ability to make sure that my investment features and characteristics are a good fit for the needs of the investor before making a recommendation to invest.
- I will create a broad pool of investors and refuse to get concentrated in a small number of investors.
- I will use leverage conservatively in appropriate amounts and for appropriate purposes.
- I will work closely with legal counsel to ensure that my fund-raising activities comply with securities regulations, including the specific exemptions from registration upon which the fund has elected to rely.
- I will attempt to only accept investors who I believe meet the following criteria:
  - accredited (or qualified as the case may be) investors only
  - good core value fit with my company
  - clear potential for additional investments over time (especially if the initial investment is small)

- □ people with a long-term time horizon (i.e., do not expect them to need their capital back in short time frames)
- □ reasonably sophisticated investors who don't require a lot of babysitting or hand holding at the basic level
- I will verify the accreditation of my investors according to the guidelines and requirements of the SEC.

Action Steps to Create Your Plan

Using my four main objectives as our guide, let me suggest some action steps you can take to start developing your written plan. Here are the steps we will take to create a coherent game plan:

1. Define (and continually redefine) your "ideal investor."

2. Develop (and refine) your "educational message." You want to create a consistent approach and theme to what message you are trying to send to your target audience.

3. Assess your current resources, and decide on any necessary bolstering. You need to be realistic about what you can actually tackle, and be prepared to add resources in the areas that you determine are most important.

4. Make your initial list of investor prospects, and create your metaphorical "garden" in whatever you use as your CRM database.[6]

5. Add to the garden consistently every day, week, and month with prequalified people you think meet the criteria of your "ideal investor."

---

6 You may need to consider (or reconsider) what CRM system you are using, as the technology side of things can be extremely helpful in your overall approach.

6. Consistently water and fertilize the garden with both marketing and sales efforts.

7. Establish a "capital-raising budget" for the coming year based on your overall choice of tactics (see below), including:

    a. Marketing

        i. Leads/lists, crowdfunding, other tactics

        ii. Execution

    b. Conference attendance

    c. Travel and entertainment

    d. Pitching/presenting at events

    e. Investor due diligence and blue sky filings

    f. Other

8. Define your specific "capital-raising game plan" (see the next section).

Capital-Raising Game Plan (CRGP)— Summary and Examples

Once you have defined your ideal investor, developed your initial educational message, assessed your resources, identified your preliminary list of investors, and created a basic budget, you are ready to create a specific, focused game plan. The remainder of this chapter is an example of the kinds of things you might include in your CRGP, all depending on your particular unique background, experience, connections, and positioning in your market. I always suggest to people to "start where you are at," meaning to leverage your existing infrastructure, contacts, connections, organizations, database, and resources before venturing out into entirely new avenues. Like the old story "Acres of Diamonds," so many people try to go out and immediately penetrate new territory in which they have no prior involvement, experience, or connections rather than concentrate on their existing plot of ground. It almost never works as well. Much better to start with whatever foundation you already have.

I have listed far more options, which I call "pillars," in my sample plan below than the actual number with which you will want to start, simply to provide a lot of ideas, examples, and possibilities. Which combination of pillars you might choose depends on your unique situation. I cannot emphasize enough the recommendation that you pick those that make the most sense for you to leverage existing relationships, connections, and infrastructure and that you focus on only a few. In actual plans we create for ourselves and our clients, each of those selected by that client—which again will be a subset of those you see here—are fleshed out in further detail with specific thoughts, steps, and plans developed and put in writing. At the end of the chapter I provide a complete example of one of them—the Existing and Former Investors and Personal Networks pillar, which I believe is the one that is most universally applicable and fruitful for all new SBRE fund managers—to give you an idea of the type of detail I suggest you develop for each pillar you choose.

Here is a summary of a sample plan of specific pillars to target your ideal investor(s), add them to your mythical "garden," communicate your educational message, and put them through your sales process.

• SAMPLE PLAN •

Below is an outline of our X-pronged approach *(I repeat—only choose how many you can realistically execute and follow through on)* to be executed more or less concurrently. These pillars are designed to be synergistic, interconnected, and continually worked in conjunction with one another:

1. Existing and Former Investors and Personal Networks
    a. Target current/existing/former investors who may consider coming to the fund.
    b. Schedule phone calls and meetings (coffee, lunch, drinks, etc.) organically and strategically (as opposed to an outbound calling campaign unless you can realistically commit to one).
    c. Target HNW acquaintances and other possible new investors from current personal network.
    d. Attempt to create ambassadors and evangelists. (You want to identify centers of influence and people who are points of leverage.)
    e. Generate referrals.
    f. Add to garden.

2. Networking Groups
    a. Join local investor/angel group and participate fully and regularly.
    b. Take on leadership role(s) as available and appropriate. (I have found that participating in the leadership structure of any organization you get involved with is very valuable.)

c. Add people to garden as appropriate.

3. Entrepreneurs / Business Owners / Executives
   a. Target business owners at or nearing an exit from their business or whose business is extremely profitable.
   b. Attend conferences and other gatherings of such people.
   c. Add to garden.

4. Wealth Managers / Registered Investment Advisors
   a. Target existing relationships.
   b. Gather referrals from investors and others to add new ones.
   c. Foster new relationships.
   d. Attend conferences.
   e. Get added to Alternative Investment Platform (AIP).
   f. Add to garden.

5. Family Offices
   a. Attend targeted conferences (Opal, IMN, iGlobal, DC Finance, FOX, etc.).
   b. Join and participate in the Family Office Group on LinkedIn.
   c. Research and target FO organizations and groups.
   d. Add to garden.

6. Foreign Investors
   a. Target any existing networks/opportunities.
   b. Target SFOs and other HNW investors internationally.
   c. Target Angel group members.
   d. Attend conferences.
   e. Add to garden.

7. Self-Directed IRA Company Relationships
   a. Attend conferences.
   b. Attend webinars.
   c. Attend lunch and learns.

8. Crowdfunding and Online Platforms
   a. Review SBREFunds.com Marketplace Listing.
   b. Target RealtyMogul, RealCrowd, CrowdStreet, Patches of Land, and others (rapidly growing and changing industry).
   c. Develop your own platform.

9. Alumni Clubs and Associations
10. Country Clubs
11. Professional Athletes (perhaps in a specific sport, area, stage of career, etc.)
12. Entertainers
13. Targeted Professional Verticals (e.g., doctors, dentists, attorneys)
14. Local Real Estate Investor Groups
15. Qualified Lists/Leads and an Education-Based Marketing Campaign
16. Effective LinkedIn Strategy
17. Small Balance Real Estate Investment Summit or Similar Event
18. Others

Lead Generation and Marketing Tactics

The following are various tactics and methods you can deploy to create quality leads and continually "water and fertilize" the garden in the key strategic areas. As with your pillars, I suggest only attempting a subset of these tactics initially, and as you make each item a part of your routine, you can add more as you move forward:

- email campaigns (a cornerstone of any good education-based marketing strategy and something to work on incorporating as soon as you can)
- face-to-face meetings (coffees, lunches, drinks, etc.) with *high-target* prospects (must be judicious as this is not very leverageable)
- launch party (an absolute must for every new fund manager in my mind)
- lunch and learns
- targeted events such as conferences, seminars, and other networking events (another must)
- press releases
- crowdfunding
- testimonials
- referrals
- webinars
- podcasts

There are many more you can do, but the idea is that you pick the ones that are most important and start there. Only add once you can commit fully to the things you have chosen. Review results frequently and adjust.

Details and Action Items—Existing and Former Investors and Personal Networks

Since this is the item we recommend universally for all new fund managers, this is one I have chosen to spend a little more time on here and share with you the type of further fleshing out I do for any of the pillars we or a client might choose. I would strongly suggest you do some version of your own "launch party" if you start a fund or a modified version if you are already running a fund and have not done such an event. Here is some of the type of language I would use in a customized capital raise strategic plan (CRSP):

Begin by consistently reaching out to any existing and former investors in your current and past investment models, as well as other members of your broader networks. Communicate and promote the launch of the new fund to these investors and the existing broader network as aggressively and as soon as possible to help create supporters and evangelists immediately upon the launch of your new fund. The objective is to create as much TOMA as you can by sharing what you are doing with as many of the people in your historical database as possible, both investors and centers of influence, both initially with your party and on an ongoing basis.

People in your networks may or may not be accredited investors, but you want to create as large a referral base as you can amongst all of the people you know and with whom you have some amount of trust already built up. You want to make them comfortable telling potential investors (such as their peers, friends, parents, in-laws, and neighbors) about what you are doing, which may create new relationships that can bear fruit over time. Add every new prequalified relationship to the garden, and begin to market to them systematically, using your education-based marketing strategy and providing value to them in advance.

Action Steps:

- ☐ Identify all possible targets (current and former), and immediately add them to the garden.
- ☐ Invite as many people as is reasonable (based on cost, budget, venue, etc.) to the launch party (expect about 50 to 60 percent of actual RSVPs to show up).
- ☐ Develop a specific strategy for the launch party that furthers your purpose of creating awareness and TOMA, which may include some or all of the following:
  - ▫ a theme for the party
  - ▫ a presentation from you about the fund, your business, why you are doing it, etc.
  - ▫ a Q&A session
  - ▫ cocktails/dinner at a local restaurant or country club
  - ▫ press coverage
  - ▫ video that you can repurpose later
  - ▫ other creative ways to maximize your time and expense of doing it
- ☐ Hold a launch party, and execute strategy.
- ☐ Send regular communications to this group of people (emails, press release, LinkedIn, announcements, etc.).
- ☐ Provide them with information and updates on a regular basis via various methods.
- ☐ Ask for testimonials when appropriate.
- ☐ Ask for referrals from this group, and add to the garden.
- ☐ Do a post party recap for those who couldn't make it.

- □ Host a webinar or other group recap.
- □ Host an intimate lunch or gathering with those who wanted to come but couldn't make it.
- □ Use your video for people who weren't there however you can.
- □ Send out a press release about the event and how successful it was afterward.
- □ Do whatever you can to carry the momentum out into your broader sphere of influence.

☐ Consider doing these periodically (anniversary party, etc.).

OTHER FACTORS IN CAPITAL-RAISING

Successful capital-raising is not based on just one thing. Rather, there are many things that combine to go into raising capital effectively, consistently, and systematically. Here are some additional ideas on several other important factors that can help your capital-raising efforts significantly if you incorporate them into your repertoire.

Marketing Materials (Slide Decks, Presentations, Tear Sheets, etc.)

You absolutely want to have some professional-looking and continually updated marketing support material for your fund and to have legal counsel review your materials before you use them in the market. The most common item is a "slide deck" or PowerPoint presentation that summarizes the key elements of the fund. You may have multiple versions of your deck that you use at different times for different purposes. You likely want to also have a one-page "tear sheet" that summarizes everything on one page, which necessarily means you will need to decide what is truly most important and interesting to your readers. If you have the resources to produce material consistently, you will end up with several versions of varying lengths that are updated regularly.

"Successful capital-raising is not based on just one thing. Rather, there are many things that combine to go into raising capital effectively, consistently, and systematically."

Make sure you have something concise that can convey to potential investors the primary information in which they are most interested, in a visual format that can be digested in no more than a few minutes. This does not take the place of your offering documents (PPM, etc.), but people are not going to want to even crack open your PPM unless they have seen something like a good deck that can capture their interest first. This does not replace effective selling, but everyone will want to see something from you up front, so you better have something professional, appealing, and compelling to let them review that will generate interest in learning more.

Follow-Up—Slide Deck, Term Sheet, PPM Log

One of the main comments we get from investors who attend our SBRE Investment Summit is that the fund managers they expressed interest in never called them to follow up after the event! Mind boggling to me, yet I see it all the time.

I suggest you maintain some type of log—a spreadsheet, in your CRM, on a yellow legal pad, something!—of any and all term sheets, slide decks, PPMs, and any other material you send out at all times. You can use this log as a follow-up mechanism to call and/or email these people to (1) get their feedback on the material—what they liked, didn't like, can improve, etc.—and (2) to determine their level of interest in investing in the fund. Very simple stuff, yet very often totally neglected.

Done right, following this process will allow you to gather that feedback, help answer any questions better in the future, learn and understand what objections or hurdles you will encounter frequently, and then attempt to incorporate appropriate improvements into the materials when it is possible to do so in order to develop an increasingly tight and powerful set of materials. It will also help you raise more money.

Sales Process

As I mentioned earlier, I believe it is very important to have a sales process that you attempt to follow for each investor who "raises his hand" and expresses interest. Even though it will never be perfect, you will want to attempt to follow the process for each investor so you know who is at what point in the process at all times. Recognize and accept that different people will move more quickly or slowly through the process. That is completely okay. The purpose of the process is to develop some predictability and reliability around who will actually close and to improve your chances of getting people to "yes."

The process may include some or all of the following:

- vetting potential investors as to the true opportunity for them to become an investor
- clarifying mutual expectations up front
- insisting upon meaningful discussions with people prior to simply sending out documents

- not being afraid to say no and/or to make no an acceptable answer to an investor (which increases the chances of them giving honest feedback)
- providing documents in a specific order for specific purposes
- obtaining commitments from people when providing documents, not necessarily to invest but that they will at least agree to schedule a time to discuss and to provide feedback one way or the other along the way so that you can continually gain better understanding about what investors like and don't like
- always asking for referrals when appropriate
- having the discipline, when "not right now" is the answer, to determine whether or not they are a viable candidate for the future (i.e., should they remain in the garden) and when would be a legitimately good time to follow up with them
- scheduling meetings selectively as appropriate (meals, events, coffee, drinks, etc.) to minimize wasted time

An excellent resource on creating and using a simple and effective sales process is the book *Let's Get Real or Let's Not Play* by Mahan Khalsa, which describes his sales process called "ORDER." I highly recommend this material to anyone serious about the idea of win-win selling who wants to develop a better process for doing it.

Testimonials[7]

I suggest you create and maintain a store of testimonials for use in your materials (slide deck, etc.). Ask for testimonials on a regular

---

7   Check with counsel about use of testimonials in your sales process. In fact, conferring with counsel on all of your marketing for appropriate disclaimers, disclosures, and other language is always a good idea.

basis when the timing is right (i.e., when they are pleased with some element of your service, offerings, follow through, help, advice, etc.). Build a catalog of these testimonials, and weave them into your materials as appropriate.

Referrals

Another area that people tend to neglect consistently is asking for referrals. Remember to ask for referrals of more people to add to your garden at appropriate times from all constituents. Increasing the number of quality "seeds" in your garden is an easy metric to measure each week that will be a predictor of future performance. Do not exert effort for referrals, but do not neglect to pay attention to their importance, and remember to ask at those appropriate times.

Weekly Capital Raise Meetings

Another thing I strongly recommend is that you hold a "capital raise" meeting each week for one hour with key capital-raising constituents (person in charge, marketing department, and anyone involved in this area). The purpose of these meetings will be to discuss overall strategy and tactics, establish priorities and action items, bring actual market data back to the group about what is working and what is not, improve processes and systems, update your strategic plan, and generally keep a tight focus on the importance of systematic, ongoing marketing and sales efforts in the capital-raising side of the business. This is easy not to do but will pay good dividends if you actually do it.

Securities Compliance

Finally, remember at all times that when you are raising capital for a 506 Regulation D pooled investment fund, you are selling securities. The consequences of violating the legal requirements surrounding the sale of securities can be severe. Therefore, I highly recommend that you engage competent legal counsel both up front and on an ongoing basis to ensure that your marketing materials, sales process, and ongoing fund-raising activities comply with all applicable securities regulations, including the specific exemptions from registration upon which your fund has elected to rely. Avoid any actions, activities, or materials that will put your exempt status in jeopardy. Work with counsel throughout the life of the fund to keep abreast of any changes in securities laws to understand your and the fund's compliance obligations.

FINAL THOUGHTS

Raising capital is a process, not an event. There is no one-size-fits-all and no panacea for good capital-raising. Unless you are a long-time fund manager and running a very large fund, you are highly unlikely to get any institutional capital. My experience is that most SBRE entrepreneurs learn to do it because it is necessary to their success—by definition—but that they do not love it or treat it with the same level of dedication and focus as the real estate acquisition, origination, and management side of their business. And raising capital in the one-deal-at-a-time or the fractional/syndication model is very different than in the pooled investment fund model. To become excellent at it requires thought, time, effort, and discipline, just like anything else in life that is worth becoming excellent at. The good news is that it is not rocket science, and any seriously committed SBRE entrepreneur who has a well-structured fund combined with disciplined under-writing can raise capital if you are determined enough to do it.

Chapter 7

General Solicitation and Advertising, 506(c) vs. 506(b), and the JOBS Act

LEGAL DISCLAIMER

As I have noted throughout this book, I am not an attorney and cannot give anyone legal advice. In this section, I am sharing with you my best understanding of certain aspects of a complicated set of rules that relate to your fundraising activities. While this understanding is based on my full immersion in those rules operationally and practically since the JOBS Act provisions were implemented, nothing I say should be construed as legal advice, and I strongly encourage you to engage competent counsel who is experienced and active in the securities field to develop a better understanding of the rules and how they apply to your unique situation.

Please also understand that much of what follows in this chapter is my opinion. Not every aspect of the current regulatory scheme is black or white, and the SBRE entrepreneur needs to make some decisions about how to interpret and apply the rules. Not even all attorneys will agree on some of the finer points of the JOBS Act and its impact on business, and both attorneys and other SBRE entrepreneurs may disagree with the opinions I voice below. For this and many other reasons, it is particularly important for you to accept what I say below for what it is—my opinion—and then form your own, after considering my points and consulting with your own qualified legal counsel.

BACKGROUND

Since 1940, anyone selling private securities that were exempt from registration has had to limit that offering strictly to people with whom they have had a "prior business relationship" (or PBR). The Investment Company Act of that year was and still is the piece of legislation that laid out what can and cannot be done in terms of how issuers—fund managers—can go about soliciting investors for the securities they are offering. For many would-be fund managers, this has been probably the most hamstringing aspect of starting their own fund—the fact that they could not openly or publicly tell anyone about that fund other than those people with whom they already had such a PBR.

When I launched my first pooled investment fund in 2001 (after more than a year and a half of trying to figure out how to do it), we, like everyone else, had to operate under these very same restrictions. The obvious question was: What constitutes a "prior business relationship" in order that one can actually speak to that person about the fund without potentially violating the law? As there was no hard and fast definition put forth by the SEC as to what constituted a PBR, it was left up to practitioners and their counsel to make such a determination. So I asked this question a lot to my securities attorney, more attorneys, other fund managers, and pretty much everyone I knew who was involved in the industry. I got a lot of different answers back, and differing schools of thought ranging from the most conservative to the very aggressive, and I took what I felt was a practical and defensible approach. We were very careful about the people we shared our fund information with, and I also witnessed many other fund managers who were not nearly as careful. For everyone, however, to one degree or another, those rules were a significant inhibitor of capital-raising.

THE JOBS ACT

Fast forward to 2012 and the JOBS Act. Among other things in that landmark legislation, the act removed the prohibition on "general solicitation and advertising" of a 506 Regulation D fund, subject to certain key conditions. All of the sudden, a fund manager could, if he was prepared to play by the new rules, tell the world that he was running a fund and seeking capital for it. We immediately recognized the potential in this development, which wasn't officially implemented until more than a year later in September 2013, and embraced the change wholeheartedly from the beginning. We therefore now have two-plus years of direct, real-world experience in general solicitation and what it has meant to us in our capital-raising efforts. We also have been engaged by various SBRE entrepreneurs in north of eighty fund-creation consulting assignments since that time, so I have discussed this topic extensively with managers all over the United States and watched their experiences firsthand as well over the past two-plus years. It is from this perspective that I share my thoughts, ideas, and opinions about this topic in the remainder of this chapter.

506(c) and 506(b)

The issuer now has a choice to elect to either utilize "general solicitation and advertising" or to not do so and instead continue to adhere to the old rules limiting solicitation to only those with whom he has a "prior business relationship." The former is called the 506(c) election and the latter the 506(b) election. The election must be made at the time the fund is launched and the blue sky filings are submitted to the SEC. It may be changed later, subject to some significant limitations—it is far easier to go from a 506(b) to a 506(c) than the other way around—but for all practical purposes, you are going to want to make your correct election at the time you launch the fund. Which one should you choose? Let me first share my personal take on the differences and implications.

The 506(b) election basically means that the issuer is going to have to adhere to the original rules prohibiting him from moving beyond those with whom he has the proverbial PBR. These rules require him to generally only accept accredited investors, although they do allow a limited number of nonaccredited investors, typically not more than thirty-five. A key element of the rules, however, is that there is *no burden of proof on the issuer as to the investor's accreditation.* It is allowable to simply accept a representation from the investor that they are in fact accredited, and this is sufficient. This of course opened the door to abuse by less-than-scrupulous issuers who would encourage investors to "check the box" that they are accredited whether they were or not, which is highly unadvisable yet unfortunately rather common.

To me, the biggest limiting factor of the 506(b) election, which, again, from 1940 until September 2013 was the only option available, is that the issuer cannot openly or publicly market, advertise, or solicit. That means no website (unless password protected for PBRs only); no print ads; no radio; no billboards; no direct mail; no cold calling; no talking about your fund to the wealthy businessman, executive, or professional you just met—basically no nothing unless you had a PBR, which, if you didn't, had to be created before you could discuss your fund. The fact that you could accept a few nonaccredited investors and, for those unscrupulous practitioners willing to wink and nod, a few more who would check a box saying they were, was not much solace to the fund manager who was struggling to figure out how to find investors for his fund outside of his current, existing network—his PBR. This is all still very true today for issuers choosing the 506(b) election.

Along comes the JOBS Act and, for the first time, the 506(c) election. No longer is the issuer limited to those with whom he has a PBR. He can now publicly advertise, market, and solicit to anyone and everyone without limitation. He can yell from the rooftops, send direct mail, cold call anyone, do an email campaign, hold a public gathering, discuss it in the press, and pretty much do anything else he wants—on *two conditions* that he did not have to meet before! One condition is that he cannot accept *any* nonaccredited investors, and the other is that the burden of proof of accreditation is on the issuer—the fund manager—and he can no longer simply accept the investor's representation that he is accredited. (I will describe my understanding of the requirements of verification below.) For now, the key point to remember is that the trade-off for being able to solicit and advertise to anyone and everyone is (1) being able to accept accredited investors only and (2) having to actually obtain reasonable proof that they are in fact accredited.

B vs. C—Which One Is Right for Me?

Clients ask me all the time whether I think the 506(c) or 506(b) is better. While there are some situations for some fund managers where I think the 506(b) election makes more sense, I believe the vast majority of the time for a new SBRE fund the 506(c) is a far superior option. I say this for several reasons.

One is that I believe it is much smarter for an issuer to only accept accredited investors anyway. Accredited investors are considered, typically rightfully, more sophisticated and knowledgeable, and therefore the laws are generally more "caveat emptor" than for nonaccredited investors. It is somewhat akin to the difference in making loans for commercial purposes instead of consumer purposes—there are just far fewer restrictions and potential regulatory pitfalls with commercial lending as compared to residential lending. The same is true when working with accredited investors only.

For us, being forced to not have any unaccredited investors was a non-issue. Long ago, we made a decision from Day 1 of Fund 1 that we would not accept *any* nonaccredited investors, even though legally we could, and if we ever sensed they were not sincere when indicating they were accredited on the necessary forms, we'd refuse to accept them. To my mind, it just wasn't worth it. That said, I realize that some new fund managers have existing investors who are not accredited and who would invest in their fund if they launched one. This is typically one of the two main reasons why new managers consider the 506(b) election. While I understand the temptation, to me this is still short-sighted thinking. Even if you have a handful of nonaccredited investors you might know who you believe would come into your fund at the outset that you would have to deny if you make the 506(c) election, they typically and by definition have less money to invest. I understand that in the beginning every investor and every dollar feels important, but in the scheme of things the total dollars you will be forgoing is typically not very much.

The second and much more important factor is that the 506(c) election allows the issuer—the fund manager—to execute an actual, legitimate, and comprehensive marketing strategy without having to work around the fundamental and severe limitation that the 506(b) rules impose by limiting you to PBRs. In the last chapter, I describe a broad and ongoing marketing and sales strategy that I recommend fund managers implement at least a portion of. Much of what I describe is not even possible or allowable in the 506(b) election, and many of these things we were never able to do until September 2013. While I certainly don't believe that just because you are able to place ads, run campaigns, and tell the world about your fund, investors will all of a sudden be beating down your door to give you money, I do believe that it better enables you to steadily disseminate your message and build awareness of your fund and your brand over time far more effectively.

Marketing alone cannot and will not get it done, of course. You still have to maintain strong underwriting disciplines (see chapter 5), have a solid and aligned capital structure (see chapter 4), administer accurately and properly, and communicate well with your investors (see chapter 8) in order to build and maintain trust. But a well-conceived, well-executed, and sustained marketing strategy makes a world of difference in systematically raising capital from investors, especially if you can figure out how to provide genuine value to them in the marketing process.

The Accreditation Verification Process

In my experience, overwhelmingly, the biggest reason people are reluctant or afraid to choose the 506(c) election is the fact that they are going to have to verify accreditation of their investors. Especially when the election was first available and to a lesser degree today, fund managers seem to be fearful of having to perform the task of verifying an investor's status as accredited. You wonder, how will they react? Will they simply not invest? Will it become an administrative burden? What constitutes acceptable verification? What happens if I think it is reasonable and the SEC doesn't? What are the consequences? These and other concerns come up repeatedly in my discussions with fund managers about whether or not to choose the 506(c) election.

"A well-conceived, well-executed, and sustained marketing strategy makes a world of difference in systematically raising capital from investors."

When it comes to acceptable verification, the SEC requires that the issuer take "reasonable" steps to verify the accredited status of purchasers of securities (investors). The SEC does not define "reasonable," much like it doesn't define "prior business relationship," and therefore allows latitude in what exactly the issuer may do. It does, however, provide a "safe harbor" provision that lays out three options to verify accreditation the issuer may choose that it agrees in advance will constitute "reasonable." The three options are summarized as follows:

1. Written confirmation from one of the following parties that they have verified the accredited status of that investor within the past ninety days:

    a.   Registered broker-dealer

    b.   Registered investment advisor

    c.   Licensed attorney or CPA

2.   Net worth verification meeting the accreditation standard (i.e., $1 million of net worth excluding the value of one's primary residence), using some combination of the following:

    a.   For assets, bank statements, brokerage statements, and other statements of securities holdings, CDs, tax assessments, and appraisal reports for real property, etc.

    b.   For liabilities, a credit report (and an attestation by the investor that there are no other material liabilities not disclosed on that credit report)

3.   Net income verification (i.e., at least $200,000 for an individual and at least $300,000 for a married couple)

    a.   Review of an individual's IRS documents (including W-2s, 1099s, K-1s, 1040s) for the most recent two years

    b.   Written certification from the investor that they reasonably expect to continue to have enough income in the coming year to qualify as accredited

Option one is by far the most widely used in my experience and the least hassle for both the issuer and the investor. We have, however, had to use options two and three in some cases. I do not dispute that having to take these additional steps to "reasonably" verify the accredited status of investors is some amount of additional administrative burden on the issuer. I do contend, however, that these are not overly burdensome requirements and that they are in fact prudent anyway. Among other things, they help avoid the problem

I previously mentioned of issuers taking a blind eye and just having investors "check the box" stating they are accredited. They provide additional information that can help a good fund manager better understand the capacity of his investors for future investments. And they can be used to assist in the sales process and getting investors to the finish line.

There is a fear among many managers that having to ask their investors for this information will turn them off and preclude an investor from investing with them. This has absolutely not been the case in my experience. Certainly we have had investors inquire why we are asking for this information, especially in the beginning, but less so today as more and more issuers are making the 506(c) election and more and more investors are becoming familiar with the process. When we explain that this is a legal requirement and that our willingness to adhere to it and our diligence in doing so is actually an indication of our commitment to quality fund management and is for their benefit as much as ours, there is little to no pushback. Certainly we have also had a few investors who became annoyed with the process, particularly when they had difficulty producing the typical information and/or their combination of assets qualifying them as accredited was more challenging to verify. There again, it actually provides us with an opportunity to demonstrate to the investor the manner in which we do business with people and generally has been a positive for us.

In short, the 506(c) election to me is a no-brainer. I find that most concerns of the fund manager around the 506(c) election are unfounded and are based primarily on a fear of the unknown. I acknowledge that I do not know what the consequences would be of failing to verify the accreditation, of having the SEC determine that the steps a manager took were not "reasonable," or of otherwise screwing up that process, but I do not think anyone else really knows either. I am not sure that there has been the first case yet of the SEC coming after someone who has elected the 506(c) option and then fallen on their face in the accreditation process (although I'm sure some fool will decide they can somehow get around doing it properly and get busted). My approach is to follow the safe harbor provisions as frequently as possible (which should be able to be done 95 percent of the time or more) and then to make sure that any other verification we do that falls outside of the safe harbor is imminently "reasonable" and that our legal counsel signs off on every one of those in advance.

I suppose it is possible to still make a mistake in this investor accreditation process, as genuine, honest mistakes can happen in life. However, my general understanding and observation in the securities world is that following the rules diligently and consistently with the guidance and advice of competent and experienced legal counsel along the way minimizes the chances of problems. The reality is that there are always more bad actors out there who deliberately and methodically mislead people, make bad decisions, and try to cover up their actions than the authorities have the bandwidth to keep up with already. Thus, I believe that it is reasonable to think that sincere and diligent attempts to comply with the rules and regulations can generally be expected to be met with favor by investors and regulators alike. The manner in which an issuer endeavors to adhere to the 506(c) election rules and the consequences of not doing so should be no exception to this general principle.

My Personal Experience

The JOBS Act passed in July 2012, but the rules were not implemented until September 2013. Having operated under the PBR rules and adhered to them as strictly as we could since our first fund was launched more than twelve years earlier, I was hyper-aware of the pending legislation and the potential removal of the general solicitation prohibition. We therefore followed it closely and had fourteen months to consider. Once the SEC finalized and effected its requirements, we were ready to pounce immediately. Since we had never taken nonaccredited investors anyway, our only implication was performing the verification requirements, which we implemented straight away. While we got some questions initially, we have not lost a single investor due to refusal to provide the necessary information. Some have threatened not to and we politely told them to feel free to pursue some other investment and they relented.

We had only launched our latest fund in April 2013, so it was still very new at the time and only had a few investors, all of whom were accredited. We had a written capital raise strategic plan, but it was considerably less robust at the outset of that fund, as we were functioning under the old 506(b) rules and could not utilize many of the tactics I articulated in chapter 6. In anticipation of what seemed like the inevitable passing of the JOBS Act during that fourteen-month quiet period, we drafted an updated version of the plan that included expanded tactics we wanted to implement once the rules went into effect. Beginning shortly after September 23, 2013, the long-worn shackles of nonsolicitation and advertising were removed.

We then expanded our overall education-based marketing campaign and increased the number of pillars we utilized to build awareness of our brand and our fund. The capital raise strategic plan is not just a concept to me but an actual document we use that describes our unique combination of pillars that we choose to use to help raise capital for our funds. To me, this marketing strategy is a long-term play. Brand awareness, credibility, and trust are only built over a significant period of time, but I do believe that one can accelerate this process and build up trust even prior to ever meeting or knowing the potential investor if your marketing strategy, tactics, and execution are solid. This was my theory at least, a theory that was never able to be tested effectively until 506(c) was an option. Finally I had the opportunity to test this theory!

Since beginning to implement our overall strategy, we have had what I consider to be excellent results. The combination of marketing pillars we have consistently executed have generated new investor prospects who, by the time they call us, are far more educated, prepared, and pre-sold on our brand than ever before. These are mostly people we have never met, never spoken to, and never knew existed who somehow stumbled onto our web presence—by googling the right combination of words, by seeing our name somewhere and looking us up online, by hearing of us from someone else they know, by seeing us at a conference, by reading a press release, or by some other unknown method—and decided to follow us and consume all that they could find online. And if you look online, you can find *a lot* on us because we produce a lot of content. They read my blogs, watch our webinars, read our press releases, check out our site, and generally spend time anonymously learning about who we are, what we do, and how we do it.

This is why I like 506(c) so much because it is how people—especially wealthy, private, and under-the-radar people—like to educate themselves and like to shop, especially in today's online world. They do not want to be sold. They do not even want to talk to you necessarily until they are comfortable enough about you to reach out on their own terms and timeline. Does the guy who can buy a Bentley or Maserati just head down to the luxury auto dealership without doing any advance homework so he can expose himself to a salesperson?

No, he looks up the cars he is interested in online—or has someone do it for him—and does some research with no one there to bother or pressure him. He reads reviews not only on the cars but also on the dealers that sell the cars. He may or may not be ready to buy right away, and the last thing he wants to do is open himself up to some salesperson who will then pester him for the next six months or more. Proper marketing and branding allows you establish authority, credibility, and trust before you even talk to people. This was impossible prior to 506(c).

An unexpected side benefit of our wider marketing strategy has been that it improves the success rate of our referral business as well. Whether it is a brand new investor we've never met or a referral from someone who already trusts us, it is much easier and less time consuming for us to systematically build valuable content we can place openly on the web that will pre-educate, pre-motivate, and pre-sell those people who meet our criteria as an "ideal investor" (see chapter 6) than it is to try to do it one person at a time on the phone or in person only if and when we have a "prior business relationship." Only after people have seen enough material to demonstrate to their own satisfaction that we are for real, that we know what we are talking about, and that we appear that we can be trusted, will they pick up the phone or write us an email to engage directly. And by doing all of this in advance, they are far better qualified and educated prospects than almost any other prospects we have.

In the past year we have had at least fifteen new investors averaging more than $250,000 each who have come to Fairway purely from our education-based marketing efforts. All of these people have found us one way or another on the Internet. We have a very wealthy and private individual from the East Coast who found us online and has invested $800,000. We have an RIA from the South who, after following our blogs for some time, visited our offices in Portland and then personally invested with us and has since recommended five other clients who have also invested. We have an extremely wealthy foreign investor who followed us for more than six months, he told us, before he decided to call. And we have multiple other similar stories from around the United States. For every one of these people, we subsequently spoke at length to them, researched them online, and made sure they met the criteria we outlined for ourselves in our own constitution (see chapter 6) in order to ensure they were a good fit for us as an investor. And finally, we verified their status as accredited using the safe harbor provisions promulgated by the SEC before we accepted their capital. You can do all of this as well with a good capital raise strategic plan and using 506(c).

FINAL THOUGHTS

Again, general solicitation and advertising is not some sort of panacea for an otherwise bad fund. As I have strongly stated throughout this book, there is a lot that goes into developing, managing, and operating a quality offering that is worthy of raising capital from investors who are abdicating control of the asset level decision making and placing their trust in a fund manager. But assuming you have done and are doing things right in the various important aspects of your pooled investment fund, the ability to not have to worry about who you are talking to about your fund and to openly market it to the wider world may be a great boon to you. It is for many diligent and hard-working fund managers around this country. Bottom line? In my opinion, done right, done consistently, and backed by competent, honest, and good faith dealings by the fund manager, general solicitation and advertising works.

Chapter 8

Effective Administration, Financial Reporting, and Investor Relations

---

I made the decision to launch my first fund in 1999. It took me until 2000 to figure out how to put the pieces together and attempt to launch. After spending $50,000 with my attorney to help me draft the documents and get the fund ready to actually start accepting money from investors and months and months of agonizing, I was finally ready to go. Or so I thought.

As we prepared to accept our first dollars, only then did I consider how I was actually going to implement, calculate, and track the economic structure my counsel had incorporated into the documents. I didn't really have any idea what the fund should look like or what the economics of it should be (see chapter 4), let alone how I would actually track it. So I started to look around for people and software that could do it. I quickly discovered there wasn't any that could efficiently do what we said we were going to do, other than manually tracking everything on spreadsheets, which I knew was not only more susceptible to errors but would also be very time consuming as the fund grew.

I finally located what I thought was some quality software that could track and administer mortgage pool funds but learned that the way I had structured the fund did not comport with its capabilities. So, much to my and my attorney's annoyance—for different reasons—I informed him that he needed to rework the offering documents so that the structure matched the software in order that I could actually track it accurately and cost-effectively. The software, as I recall, cost me about $10,000 (not including the ongoing quarterly fees), and the changes to the PPM and related offering documents necessary to conform to the software cost me another $15,000 or so with my counsel, precious working capital I did not want to be spending on more changes to my legal documents.

In short, like most SBRE entrepreneurs trying to realize the dream of transcending the one-deal-at-a-time model and raise capital more efficiently and in larger quantities, I completely underestimated the importance of what it was going to take to track the fund's performance, account for both the deals and the investors coming and going at random intervals, and otherwise professionally monitor and administer the fund. This element is so often an afterthought, and people end up having to piece together ways and means to try to track a structure they are not sure why they chose in the first place. This can work when the fund is very small, but it gets very complicated and time consuming (not to mention expensive) very quickly.

The final piece of the puzzle for an SBRE entrepreneur who wants to be able to raise capital successfully on an ongoing basis is to make sure that he can perform timely, accurate, and effective administration of the fund's activities and performance and then to communicate this information in a meaningful way at frequent, regular intervals to his investors. To do this requires first to know how to actually do it, which is usually as completely foreign to new fund managers as it was to me initially and secondly to develop and implement processes, systems, and checklists (or to hire a third party cost effectively who already has those things).

"The final piece of the puzzle for an SBRE entrepreneur who wants to be able to raise capital successfully on an ongoing basis is to make sure that he can perform timely, accurate, and effective administration of the fund's activities and performance and then to communicate this information in a meaningful way at frequent, regular intervals to his investors."

There are three components to effective administration that I touch upon in this chapter. Each has much more depth and nuance to them than I am able to cover here, but this overview will hopefully provide you with enough understanding of what needs to be considered in advance so that you can avoid making the same mistakes I did when I launched that first fund more than fifteen years ago. The three critical components of effective fund administration are (1) accurate accounting, (2) timely reporting, and (3) good investor communication. I have placed these in what I believe is the order of their importance inasmuch as each flows from the previous one. Let's discuss each of these in more detail.

ACCURATE TRACKING, ACCOUNTING, AND SHARE PRICE CALCULATION

In the past several years, I have advised on, administered, invested in, considered investing in, reviewed, and/or encountered literally hundreds of SBRE funds around the United States. In doing so, I have had the opportunity to witness how people implement their fee and economic structure in actual practice, how they track and monitor the activities in the fund, and how they account for the performance of their assets, their income and expenses, and their investor capital accounts. One thing I can say for sure is that *it is all over the map!* Too often it is indecipherable, inaccurate, or simply being done downright improperly, mostly without the manager (and the investors) even realizing it. There are those who do it brilliantly, for sure, but that is the exception rather than the rule, and most find this area to be confusing, burdensome, and time consuming.

The challenge people have springs from the fact that deals in a pooled investment fund do not stand on their own as they do in the one-deal-at-a-time or fractional/syndication models but rather are all comingled with one another. Deals that get originated or acquired will go full cycle at various intervals throughout the week, month, and year. At the same time, investors come into—and in the case of an open-ended fund, may go out of—the fund at *different* points in time. How do you calculate and allocate income and expenses properly when both the assets and the investors are coming and going at various, random times? Most have no idea how to do this accurately. It helps a great deal to have structured the fund up front in a way that contemplates all of this, as it then makes it far easier to accurately manage, although still not a piece of cake for most managers who by nature tend to be salespeople and dealmakers more so than accountants and administrators.

In most funds, investors who provide the capital are purchasing shares of the entity that *is* the fund and thus are becoming equity owners of that fund entity. This means that you as the manager have to determine what price the investor is paying for the shares he is buying and to do so consistent with all applicable laws and accounting regulations, as well as your PPM and other offering documents. The manner in which an SBRE fund operates is basically the same as a mutual fund in the equities market. That is, the price of a share of that mutual fund is determined by the collective underlying price of each of the securities comprising that mutual fund. In a publicly traded and completely liquid mutual fund, this is an easy calculation, since each of the underlying securities has a price that is quoted at every second on a public exchange. In a private SBRE fund, however, there is no such public price or market for either the shares of the fund or the underlying assets inside that fund. So what is the price of a share of a given fund at any given moment in time? The answer is, it depends on what value is being ascribed to the underlying assets, and that value can sometimes be quite subjective.

Let me give you an example. Let's say we have a fix-n-flip, open-ended fund with a fluctuating share price (which it should have if it is an open-ended fund and it was set up properly). The underlying assets are homes that are being bought, rehabbed, and sold. There are many homes coming and going at all times because our manager is busy and successful and does significant deal volume. He buys a home for $100,000 on January 1 with a budget of $25,000 for rehab, and he expects to sell it for $200,000, let's say. On March 31—the end of the accounting period and the point in time when he is going to subscribe new investors—the $25,000 has been spent, the home has been rehabbed (it is beautiful, by the way!), the market is still strong, and the manager has listed the home for $210,000, hoping to get it but still anticipating his initial ARV of $200,000. The property has been completed, thus removing the rehab and construction risk of that deal, but it hasn't yet sold on that date, thus leaving primarily only the marketing risk, which in the current market conditions the manager judges to be minimal based on recent comparable sales, overall time on market of similar properties, personal experience with other homes in the fund, etc. So the question is, what is the value of that asset for the purposes of determining the price of a share to the investors he is going to subscribe on April 1?

Well, his cost basis is $125,000. The list price is $210,000, and he believes the market value is $200,000. The $75,000 difference between the believed market value and the cost basis has been *created* but not yet *realized*. Who took the risk of that asset? The answer is the investors who were in the fund during the time the value was created. That would lead us to believe that they should receive that value. But the property hasn't sold yet and thus there is no cash in exchange for that value. The manager can "mark to market" that asset, which would effectively increase the share price for the new investors to reflect the value that has been created and reward the investors who took the risk during the time of value creation. But what if the market tanks shortly thereafter and the property only sells for $175,000? There are many such scenarios that could impact investors one way or another. The point is that there is no perfect answer. In a best-case scenario, the manager understands all of this deeply and takes a measured, thoughtful, and consistent approach to how he treats the valuation of that asset, with an eye toward its effect on share price and ultimately to both new and existing investor benefit (or detriment).

This is a very difficult concept for most managers to completely grasp. It took me many years to fully understand it and to appreciate its true importance. Most investors frankly do not understand this any better than the managers do. As a result, share prices are often quoted at a fixed price, which may or may not really reflect the true underlying asset values. This is all disclosed—or should be—in the offering documents as a risk factor inherent in such offerings, so investors should understand that this—as well as many other factors—is a fundamental risk to the investment. Merely disclosing such a risk does not mean, however, that a manager who wants to differentiate himself from the rest and make his offering more attractive to capital sources shouldn't educate himself thoroughly so as to understand deeply how this works and why. If he will take the time and effort to do so, he will be able to (1) account for it as diligently as possible in order to treat investors as equally and fairly as he can and (2) demonstrate to his investors that he is more conscious of this dynamic and thoughtful of its implications to them than most other SBRE fund managers and thus is more worthy of their trust and their investment.

In addition to accurately determining the value of each of the underlying assets in a fund and endeavoring to produce a fair and accurate share price as consistently as possible, there is also great confusion around the allocation of income and expenses. In many if not most real SBRE fund asset models, the underlying assets may have income that has accrued or been earned but has not yet been paid. Expenses may have been paid but need to be amortized over some time period. How and when the income and expenses get recognized is important because investors may be coming and/or going during these periods and may or may not be allocated their appropriate share of either or both. Depending on how the manager is tracking and accounting for these income and expenses, it may benefit or be to the detriment of certain investors depending on when they come or go.

For example, it is often more advantageous for investors to come into a closed-ended (and sometimes even open-ended) fund at the very end of the raise period or of a quarterly (or annual) period because they will get allocated income earned from the entire previous period even though their capital was only deployed and therefore at risk for the last day or week of that period, thus increasing their return for that period (and incrementally reducing it for the other investors). Such situations are very common, and most managers—and investors—do not understand and appreciate these nuances. Mostly they are relatively small dollar amounts, but in certain cases they can be quite significant. As an investor in other funds, we pay very close attention to how aware managers are of such issues and how they treat and apply them.

There are other similar (if perhaps less impactful) issues that regularly arise in the operation and accounting of pooled investment funds that are not well understood by most managers or their investors that nevertheless impact performance of both the fund and the individual investors inside those funds. I haven't even discussed tax return preparation (K-1s are always near and dear to HNW investors' hearts and minds), audits, and other important elements of fund administration. It is beyond the scope of this chapter (and my expertise—please see A Word of Caution, page 7) to detail them all. Rather, the point to remember is that accurate administration, accounting, and application of proper fund accounting principles is an important yet oft-misunderstood and highly frustrating aspect of SBRE funds that can impact investors in those funds. You can set yourself apart and make yourself more attractive to capital if you understand these issues and principles, apply them consistently, and demonstrate to your investors that you are ahead of the curve on this front. It rightfully engenders confidence and trust in them and helps you raise capital more consistently through additional investments and referrals from current investors.

TIMELY REPORTING AND GOOD INVESTOR COMMUNICATION

Flowing logically from the first topic, reporting and communicating relevant financial and other information to your investors in a timely and consistent fashion is the next area that, if you master it, will pay ongoing dividends to your capital-raising efforts. There is nothing more powerful for you in those efforts than being able to get strong endorsements and referrals from your current, existing investors. To do this, you will have to earn it, not only with your performance, which of course is wildly important (see chapter 5), but also with the accuracy, the depth, the quality, and the frequency of your communication with them.

Good reporting should be timely (meaning you provide the information shortly after the close of a given period), thorough (meaning you provide enough information for them to understand what is happening), and regular (meaning you should develop appropriate rhythms they can come to expect rather than doing it randomly whenever you can find the time to pull away from the asset side of the fund operations). I completely understand how difficult it can be to spend time doing this when there is so much other work to do on the origination, acquisition, asset management, and disposition side of the equation. But if you want to cultivate happy investors, which is one of the most powerful things you can do to enhance your future capital-raising efforts, you need to make a commitment to getting excellent at timely reporting and good investor communication.

I recommend creating a calendar for yourself that lays out in advance the rhythms that you are going to develop and follow. Your communication should include several elements, each of which may be done at different intervals but which should be decided upon and executed according to a schedule. Generally I recommend quarterly as a frequent enough but not too frequent rhythm that balances the practical time constraints of the manager with the needs of the investor to stay abreast of what is happening. This Communication Checklist is a good guideline.

Communication Checklist

- ☐ making distributions (monthly, quarterly, or other)
- ☐ providing capital account statements (perhaps along with distributions)
- ☐ holding conference call updates (monthly or quarterly)
- ☐ providing (typically quarterly and sometimes less frequently) written fund and asset performance updates that have been reviewed by counsel
- ☐ providing financial statements
- ☐ holding shareholder/investor meetings (annually typically, perhaps semi-annually)
- ☐ scheduling individual investor calls, meetings, etc. (case by case, but develop a strategy)
- ☐ sending email updates (varies)
- ☐ updating investor portals
- ☐ other

The better the job you do at communicating honestly, openly, thoroughly, and frequently, the happier your investors will be and the more likely they will be to add to their investment and/or recommend others. Obviously returns and performance are important. However, my overwhelming experience is that investors care more about knowing what is happening than they do about results (within reason). A manager producing a 9 percent return and communicating as I suggest will get better capital-raising results from his existing investor base than a manager producing a 13 percent return but never communicating with his investors. They will become suspicious and wonder what is going on, often believing that sooner or later the 13 percent is too good to be true unless the manager clearly explains how, why, and his expectations for the future in some regular way.

You will also want to determine *how* to communicate with your investors. What media will you use, in what situations, and for what purposes? Will you send distribution checks in the mail, or will you deposit money electrically via ACH? Will you send your quarterly letter in the mail, or will you send it via email? Will you send capital account statements, tax returns, and audited—which I suggest you will want and if not audited, then at least reviewed or compiled—financial statements in the mail or via secure email, or will you upload them to a password-protected investor portal to which you give access to your investors? Will you hold conference calls via phone, Skype, webinar, or other format? Will you record it and make it available to investors who missed the call? If so, how will you distribute it? And so on.

As reality sets in on your life as a fund manager, you understand that there are only so many hours in the day and that you must prioritize. Understanding that investor communication is important, you want to try to do as much as you can to create rhythms they can come to expect (humans like predictability). But you also want to do it in a way that doesn't create a ton of time-consuming, repetitive work that is required on an ongoing basis. Therefore, you will want to create mechanisms that enable you to do things regularly and thoroughly but also efficiently and cost effectively. An investor portal is an excellent way to provide information to all of your investors but that only requires that you upload the information once each time you want to communicate. Anything that goes to all of them can be uploaded here, such as quarterly letters; fund financial statements; fund tax returns; offering documents and supplements; other managerial documents or policies such as underwriting criteria, stated value methodology, and operational procedures; or anything else you might want to make available. This is cheap and efficient, and often just knowing it is available is enough to make investors feel comfortable and confident that the manager is actively providing information.

Finally, I also suggest making a commitment to yourself that you will return phone calls and inquiries from existing investors, no matter how much you might have going on or how much you feel it may be repeating what you have already communicated, as rapidly as possible. Another suggestion is to communicate negative information or bad news just as openly, frequently, and thoroughly as you would positive information. Often a manager's tendency will be to withhold negative information for fear of losing investors, increasing redemptions, or otherwise having bad things happen. They tend to wait too long to face reality and to communicate that reality to investors, and it can then get harder and harder to ever do it, especially if conditions and results deteriorate. This is when good communication can be most important and most effective and separates the most trustworthy managers from the rest.

FINAL THOUGHTS

Doing this component of fund management well can be one of your best capital-raising tools. You have to work very hard to get investors to come into your fund in the first place. You don't want to blow the opportunity to impress them once they are in it by messing up their statements, communicating sporadically or not at all, not being able to provide important and meaningful information, and/or not creating opportunities to interact with them (and to get them to interact with each other). This seems obvious, but making these mistakes is all too common. I completely understand why, as I have not always been the best at these things either. You get busy with deals, with closings, with project management, and with the fund's assets themselves. Frankly, this is what you enjoy doing and what you are good it. Accounting, tracking, preparing financials, writing letters, creating and documenting policies—these are not typically the strong suit of the SBRE entrepreneur. The good news is you can very cost effectively outsource a good deal of these activities. You should commit to developing competency and even mastery of the rest over time. If you underwrite and manage assets well, combining good reporting and communication will pay big dividends in your capital-raising efforts over time.

Conclusion

The combination of opportunities, constraints, and issues that faces you as an enterprising SBRE entrepreneur is not well studied, documented, or addressed. The overwhelming majority of information and education available is designed and targeted toward institutional sponsors and investors. Unfortunately, much of this material is simply not applicable to the SBRE entrepreneur and in fact is often the precise opposite of what works in reality, in my experience. Certainly there are lessons to be learned and material to be applied from the institutional world, but this information must be filtered and translated so that it does not simply confuse the issues at hand and lead you down an endless trail that does not take you where you want to go. This is nothing short of an epidemic for SBRE entrepreneurs.

The institutional world and the SBRE world are like parallel universes that live side by side and have different rules, laws, and gravitational pulls. If you live in the SBRE world and you try to operate by the institutional rules, you are likely to frustrate yourself repeatedly. You would be wise to study their rules but at the same time realize that they are not to be taken literally in the land of SBRE. Given their ubiquity in the media, at industry conferences, and pretty much wherever you turn, it is hard not to succumb to these ideas, which I consider to be dogma treated as inviolable by the institutional people who promulgate them—many of whom have lived only in that universe their entire lives and cannot conceive of anything else—and which are often blindly accepted by unquestioning SBRE entrepreneurs who see the many extra zeroes on the end of the institutional deal sizes and assume they must be correct.

I just finished attending a conference in Laguna, California, this week and spent the better part of three days listening to panelists discuss a range of topics on private real estate funds. Once again, the great majority of the opinions, experiences, and advice I heard being dispensed to new and emerging managers, although perhaps perfectly suited to fund managers attempting to raise capital from institutional investors, was totally off target for most SBRE entrepreneurs. I always seem to be a dissonant voice on any panel on which I speak because I am invariably the only one on it from the SBRE universe and not its parallel constellation. Fortunately, there always seems to be a subset, often even a silent majority, of conference attendees for whom my opinions and observations resonate because they intuitively understand that many of the things they have been hearing somehow just don't make sense to them or have failed to work for them repeatedly. I have shared many of these opinions and observations with you in this book and hope that they resonate with you, too. If they do, I predict you will attain much greater success and fulfillment in your small balance real estate enterprise and do a better job of systematically attracting capital to your business.

Bringing Mastery to Small Balance Real Estate Funds

Fairway America, LLC is widely recognized as the leader of the Small Balance Real Estate (SBRE) investment community. Fairway provides a comprehensive range of services and opportunities to SBRE entrepreneurs, fund managers, syndicators, private lenders, and other dealmakers, including fund creation and advisory, fund administration, capital raise strategy, online listing opportunities, live investor events, and more. Fairway also helps educate investors about the SBRE space and, through a variety of mechanisms, helps introduce investors to SBRE investment opportunities.

Visit www.fairwayamerica.com or call 503-906-9100 to learn more about Fairway or the SBRE investment community.

SBRE Entrepreneurs: If you are a real estate entrepreneur with a quality strategy and attractive risk-adjusted returns and are looking to start or administer a fund, capitalize your existing fund or syndications, or have other questions about SBRE, we want to talk to you. We give you the tools, knowledge, confidence, and support you need to systematically attract capital to your small balance real estate business. You can find more information and resources at www.fairwayamerica.com/advisory/.

Investors: Fairway America operates two proprietary 506 Reg. D funds, Fund VI and Fund VII. It also introduces investors to other SBRE investment opportunities through its online portal and live events. You get preferred access to expertise, information, and opportunities from the trusted authority in the space. To learn more about these investment opportunities, we encourage you to visit www.SBREfunds.com.